A Contribution to the Empirics of Economic and Human Development

Göttinger Studien zur Entwicklungsökonomik
Göttingen Studies in Development Economics
Herausgegeben von/ Edited by Hermann Sautter und/and Stephan Klasen

Bd./Vol. 27

PETER LANG
Frankfurt am Main · Berlin · Bern · Bruxelles · New York · Oxford · Wien

Sebastian Vollmer

A Contribution to the Empirics of Economic and Human Development

PETER LANG
Internationaler Verlag der Wissenschaften

Bibliographic Information published by the Deutsche Nationalbibliothek
The Deutsche Nationalbibliothek lists this publication in the Deutsche Nationalbibliografie; detailed bibliographic data is available in the internet at <http://www.d-nb.de>.

Zugl.: Göttingen, Univ. Diss., 2009

Gratefully acknowledging the support of the
Ibero-Amerika-Institut für Wirtschaftsforschung, Göttingen.

Cover illustration by Rolf Schinke

D 7
ISSN 1439-3395
ISBN 978-3-631-58793-5

www.peterlang.de

Meinen Eltern

Editor's Preface

This book by Sebastian Vollmer contributes to the empirical literature on economic and human development from a range of different perspectives.

The first three essays are concerned with the world income distribution, studying its shape and evolution over time. The first essay presents a new parametric test for bimodality of a density. The test is more powerful than its nonparametric counterparts given that certain parametric assumptions are reasonable. The essay also includes an application of this new methodology to the cross-sectional distribution of per capita log GDP across EU regions from 1970 to 1993. In fact, the test is able to identify convergence from two modes to one mode in this data set, while alternative tests are not able to do so.

The second essay challenges the famous Twin Peaks claim by Danny Quah concerning the shape of the global income distribution. Vollmer argues that the number of modes of a distribution is not robust towards rescaling of the data (for example taking logs). Although information on the number of modes might be useful for proper visualization of the data, it is not appropriate to derive conclusions concerning the number and development of convergence clubs. The empirical model of Vollmer's essay overcomes these shortcomings, and it turns out that the world's cross-country income distribution consists of three components since 1976 (and two components beforehand). The three components are diverging since 1976, i.e. the richest component is growing faster than the middle component and the middle component is growing faster than the poorest component both in relative and absolute terms. In a posterior analysis probabilities of belonging to a certain component in a given year are assigned to each country.

In the third essay, Vollmer focuses on a related, but fundamentally different question, namely the evolution of the global income distribution where the units of analysis are individuals rather than countries. The essay is original because of its unprecedented detail by generating global growth incidence curves for given time periods and also global regions which allows identifying the pro-poorness of past growth. Moreover, the essay finds that the global income distribution has experienced convergence since 1970, as the bottom-middle part of the distribution grew the fastest. These findings go hand in hand with declining poverty rates and absolute number of poor with Sub-Saharan Africa and Latin America being exceptions. The most remarkable decline took place during the late 1970s and early 1980s. Most notably are the significant positive changes in the regional distributions of South Asia and East Asia. Overall global inequality declined slightly due to a decrease in between country inequality, which however is counteracted by a slight increase of within country inequality.

In the fourth essay, Vollmer analyzes the welfare effects of recently negotiated Economic Partnership Agreements between the European Union and African countries. The essay provides some background information on how the Economic Partnership Agreements evolved and then turns to a standard trade model in order to estimate whether consumption and trade creation effects outweigh trade diversion effects. The essay extends the literature in this field significantly by estimating elasticities of import demand from highly disaggregated data and applying the actual negotiated tariff reduction rates in the estimation of the agreement's welfare effects. It is a strength of the essay to use the empirical results for an extensive discussion of policy conclusions.
In the fifth essay, Vollmer investigates whether democracy promotes the non-income dimensions of human development. The theoretical argument focuses both on quantitative aspects in form of redistribution as well as qualitative aspects such as accountability and needs oriented policies in democracies. Democracy is identified to have positive and highly significant impact on human development in a panel framework controlling for GDP per capita, inequality, fractionalization, HIV among other variables. Interestingly, the interaction effects of democracy with GDP per capita, inequality, fractionalization and education turn out to be insignificant or not robust. This implies that democracy itself is important for human development and less the circumstances under which it occurs.
These essays all make important contributions to the empirical literature on economic and human development and I am pleased that this book has been included in our series of studies on development economics.

Prof. Stephan Klasen, Ph.D.
Göttingen, July 2009

Author's Preface

Writing a dissertation is not possible without the support and friendship of many people. I wish to express my heartfelt gratitude to the following people, without whom the writing of this dissertation would not have been possible.

First of all I would like to thank my supervisor, Professor Stephan Klasen, for accepting me as a doctoral student and giving me the opportunity to write this thesis. He gave me a great deal of freedom to organize my work as I wished and, at the same time, he was extremely supportive whenever I had a question (and has given great input and ideas to whatever I have asked him). I would also like to thank my second advisor, Professor Stefan Sperlich. He was also very supportive and took the time to discuss methodological issues whenever I had a question. I would also like to thank both for giving me academic guidance beyond this thesis.

My colleagues made the work in Göttingen and at the World Bank very enjoyable. They enriched my life in many different ways, some as co-authors, others through comments on my essays, collaboration, or moral support, or simply via interesting conversations during lunch breaks, coffee breaks, or with a drink in the evening. There are too many to name them all but in particular I would like to thank Michaela Beckmann, Souleymane Coulibaly, Uwe Deichmann, Indermit Gill, Johannes Gräb, Melanie Grosse, Carola Grün, Isabel Günther, Kenneth Harttgen, Dierk Herzer, Hajo Holzmann, Andreas Kopp, Steffen Kröhnert, Inmaculada Martínez-Zarzoso, Mark Misselhorn, Felicitas Nowak-Lehmann, Jan Priebe, Ramona Rischke, Katharina Scholz, Julian Weisbrod, and Maria Ziegler.

I gratefully acknowledge a Georg-Christoph Lichtenberg scholarship from the Center of Statistics at the University of Göttingen. This scholarship gave me the economic freedom to focus on my statistical education and on research. I also acknowledge conference travel grants from the University of Göttingen, the Deutsche Forschungsgemeinschaft, the Spanish Ministry of Education and Science, the Universitätsbund Göttingen e.V., and the Deutsche Bundesbank.

My sincere thanks go to Clive Bell, Matthias Busse, David Canning, Mark Dincecco, Steven Durlauf, Michael Grimm, Carola Grün, Dierk Herzer, Birgit Hofmann, Rainer Klump, Tatyana Krivobokova, Branko Milanovic, Sanjay Reddy, Xavier Sala-i-Martin, Martin Schlather, Evita Schmieg, Michael Ward, Walter Zucchini, and anonymous referees for helpful comments or discussions on one or more of my five essays. All of them provided extremely valuable assistance for improving this dissertation.

In addition, comments from participants of seminars in Göttingen, Hannover, Bologna, Erfurt, Lüneburg, and the following conferences helped to improve this dissertation: Research in In-

ternational Economics and Finance (Rome 2007), Research Committee on Development Economics of the German Economic Association (Göttingen (2007), German Economic Association (Munich 2007), Institutional and Social Dynamics of Growth and Distribution (Pisa 2007), International Society for Comparative Economic Studies (São Paulo 2008), Global Economic Analysis (Helsinki 2008), International Economic Association (Istanbul 2008), Far Eastern and South Asian Meeting of the Econometric Society (Singapore 2008), European Economic Association (Milan 2008), American Economic Association (San Francisco 2009), Sir Arthur Lewis Institute of Social and Economic Studies (Barbados 2009), Econometric Society (Boston 2009), Dynamics, Economic Growth and International Trade (Los Angeles 2009). These helpful participants have my sincere gratitude.
Finally, my biggest thanks go to my family and my friends. They always trusted in me and without their persistent support and encouragement I would not have been able to finish this dissertation.

Sebastian Vollmer
Hannover, June 2009

Contents

List of Tables

List of Figures

Introduction

It is a difficult task to write an introduction to a collection of essays which come from separate areas of economics. The essays cover a rather broad range of topics. Essay 1 is a methodological contribution to the analysis of densities and distributions. Essays 2 and 3 apply state-of-the-art parametric statistical techniques to analyze the world income distribution from both cross-country and individual perspectives. Essay 4 concerns the welfare effects of recently negotiated trade agreements between the European Union and African countries. Finally, Essay 5 addresses some interesting correlations between the non-income dimensions of human development and democracy. Due to the breadth of the topics, this is not an introduction in the classical sense, introducing the field of research treated by the essays, but rather more of an overview. Below, the main results of each essay are highlighted, followed by an explanation of how the essay contributes to its field of research.

Essay 1: A Likelihood Ratio Test for Bimodality in Two-Component Mixtures

This essay proposes a parametric test for bimodality based on the likelihood principle by using two-component mixtures. (Bimodality means that the density function of a distribution has two modes.) The hypothesis that the density function only has one mode is tested against the alternative that it has two modes. The test uses explicit characterizations of the modal structure of such mixtures in terms of their parameters. The asymptotic distribution of the proposed test is analyzed. Analyzing the modality of the distribution of a random sample is an important problem, particularly for proper graphical visualization of the data. In particular, it is important to decide whether modes present in a certain fit are merely sampling artifacts or whether they are actual features of the underlying density. (We will see in the second essay, however, that it might be misleading to rely upon the number of modes alone when analyzing a distribution.)

The essay is foremost a methodological contribution to the literature which already comprises two major tests for the number of modes, the test by Silverman (1981) and the dip test by Hartigan and Hartigan (1985). Both tests are nonparametric and therefore applicable to more flexible settings than the likelihood ratio test (LRT). The finite sample performance of the LRT is investigated in a simulation study and compared to Silverman's test and the dip test. The simulation confirms that the LRT is keeping its level and has a greater power than either Silverman's test or the dip test if the principle distributional assumptions are fulfilled. The nonparametric tests also work well for cases where the distributional assumptions of the LRT are violated. Hence, this essay provides a new statistical tool which is more powerful for certain types of applications than existing techniques. An additional highlight of the LRT compared to the nonparametric tests is that the LRT is also applicable to mixtures of multivariate normal distributions and the von Mises distribution (the so-called circular data), cases for which no tests for bimodality have to date been available.

The final section of the essay is an empirical application with real data. The modal structure of the cross-sectional distribution of per capita log GDP across EU regions from 1977 to 1993 is investigated using mixtures. While these mixtures clearly involve two components over the whole time period, the resulting distributions evolve from bimodality toward unimodality at the end of the seventies. This example proves how useful the LRT is in some settings because Silverman's test is not able to identify the transition from bimodality to unimodality in this case due to its lack of power in such settings.

Essay 2: Twin Peaks or Three Components?

What is it that makes some countries so much more prosperous on average than others? This and related questions are at the heart of the second essay. The topic of this essay is the world's cross-country distribution of GDP per capita and its evolution from 1970 to 2003. It contributes to a large body of empirical growth literature which tests for absolute and conditional convergence among the countries of the world (Barro 1991 and Quah 1996a, among others), but also to a more theoretical branch of the growth literature which predicts multiple equilibria in the world's cross-country income distribution (Quah 1996b and Galor 1996, among others). Quah describes these equilibria as emerging *Twin Peaks*, while Galor (1996) introduces the concept of multiple steady-state equilibria without any restriction on the number of steady states. Bianchi (1997) was the first to formally test for the number of modes in the world's cross-country distribution of income using the method by Silverman (1981). He confirmed the predictions of Quah (1996). Paap and Dijk (1998) model the cross-country distribution of income as parametric mixture; however, they obtain the number and type of mixture components merely by visual inspection and not by statistical inference.

This essay challenges the *Twin Peaks* claim. It can easily be shown that the number of modes is not invariant of the scale; this means that the number of modes might change when switching to the logarithmic scale from a regular scale. Such a property is extremely undesirable for this type of economic analysis. Since the scale of GDP per capita does not alter the economic characteristics of a country, it should therefore not be responsible for the assignment of a country to one convergence club or the other. Though the number of modes is of interest in a different context, one can argue that the concept of *Twin Peaks* is misleading and does not help to identify convergence clubs.

Thus, the essay proposes to model the cross-country income distribution as a mixture of normal distributions. The number of components is determined by recently published modified likelihood-ratio tests by Chen et al. (2001, 2004) and Chen and Kalbfleisch (2005), as well as model-selection criteria. The parameters of the normal components are fitted from the data. One advantage of this approach is that the components in the mixture have a clear interpretation as income groups or convergence clubs and, in contrast to modes of the density, their number does not depend upon the scale of the data. It turns out that the cross-country distribution of GDP per

capita consists of two components from 1970 to 1975. In 1976 a third component emerges and becomes progressively more pronounced with increasing statistical significance until 2003.
The model allows a so-called posterior probability to be assigned to each country. The posterior probability describes the probability of a country belonging to a certain component (interpreted as convergence club) in a given year. This concept takes into account the fact that it does not make much sense to assign countries to income groups based on their GDP per capita, alone, but rather to show the different possibilities of group affiliations since GDP per capita alone does not provide enough information about the future growth path of a country. Looking at the development of each component's mean income over time leads to some interesting observations. The mean income of the poorest component had a growth rate of 0 from 1976 to 2003, whereas the middle component had an average annual growth rate of 1.2 percent, and the richest component had an average annual growth rate of 2.2 percent during the same period. This implies that the three components were diverging both in absolute and in relative terms.
A drawback to this approach is that the σ parameters of the normal distributions in the mixture must be equal because there are no tests for unequal σ parameters available to date (at least not for two of three components). Another justification for this restriction is the fact that the fit of the richest component would be extremely narrow if one allowed for unequal σ parameters. The fit would be so narrow around a group of high-income European countries that the richest countries (in particular the United States) would be excluded by this component and instead captured by the longer tail of the middle component. Hence, the restriction of equal σ parameters forces the richest component to include the richest countries, which makes much more sense for economic interpretation. Nevertheless, one has to admit that the assumption of equal σ parameters is a restriction of the model.

Essay 3: Income Distribution Dynamics and Pro-Poor Growth
The second essay shows divergence of three components in the cross-country income distribution. About one third of the world's countries are caught in a poverty trap without any economic growth. Nevertheless, official statistics from the World Bank show a rapid decline of poverty during the given period. How are these disparate facts reconcilable? The cross-country analysis also shows that particular populous countries grew quickly enough to catch up to richer countries; in fact, China, India, and Indonesia belong to the group of the largest gainers, as measured by differences in their posterior probabilities. While the cross-country perspective is useful to analyze growth, convergence, and income polarization, it fails to address size and income inequality within countries. Thus, a different perspective on world income distribution is necessary to further explore questions of welfare, inequality, and poverty.
From an individual perspective, world income distribution is an appealing topic for current research. A better understanding of the participatory nature of growth is clearly relevant for the world community when it comes to meeting the Millennium Development Goals of halving global poverty and hunger by 2015. There is an ongoing debate in the literature about how global growth, inequality, and poverty should be measured. National accounts or survey data? Micro or macro data? Measure poverty based upon income or upon consumption? These and other questions are discussed by Ravallion (2003), Deaton (2005), and Milanovic (2006), among others. Two main concepts are applied to obtain estimates of world income distribution: The first

approach, labeled Concept 2 by Milanovic (2006), combines national accounts income data with household survey inequality data to derive a global income distribution. The second approach, labeled Concept 3 by Milanovic, 2006, is purely based upon income and inequality data from household surveys.

Milanovic (2002) and Sala-i-Martin (2006) are the most important contributions to literature which actually estimates world income distribution. Milanovic (2002) estimates it based upon household survey data, alone, whereas Sala-i-Martin (2006) combines GDP data from the Penn World Tables with inequality data from the World Institute of Development Economics Research (WIDER) data set. Clearly, Milanovic's approach is the most adequate for analyzing world income distribution for recent years, but it is less useful for analyzing the dynamics of the past 40 years; only for recent years is there a sufficient amount of survey data available and it is also only recently that major efforts have been made to make household surveys more comparable over space and time. Thus, although the approach of Milanovic is, in principle, superior to other approaches, it cannot answer all questions of interest about world income distribution.

This essay takes a similar approach to Sala-i-Martin (2006); GDP data from the Penn World Tables are combined with improved Gini data based on the WIDER data set. Sala-i-Martin (2006) uses quintile and decile data to obtain estimates for national income distributions based on non-parametric techniques. One could argue that the data at hand are not sufficient to fully exploit these techniques; in fact, Sala-i-Martin (2006) claims to be more precise and sophisticated than is justified by the data. This essay thus exploits the information in the data by a simpler methodology–national income distributions are modeled parametrically as log-normally distributed. Although this is a no-progress approach from a methodological point of view, one can nevertheless argue that it is as good as Sala-i-Martin's approach, and, moreover, it is useful for answering questions regarding growth incidence and inequality decomposition which have not yet been treated by Sala-i-Martin (2006) or Milanovic (2002).

The results show that the past 34 years have witnessed a strong global income convergence accompanied by a drastic decline in global income inequality and poverty. Noticeably, overall inequality declined because of diminishing inequality between countries, while economic inequality within countries increased. Furthermore, the analysis of growth-incidence curves shows that the bottom-middle part of the income distribution experienced above average percentile growth rates, which growth explains the existing global income convergence. In particular, the late 1970s and early 1980s are characterized by high global rates of pro-poor growth, initiating the rapid decline of global poverty rates.

A regional decomposition of the data reveals that, in particular, the extraordinary growth record of East Asia and South Asia, which includes the two population heavyweights China and India, accounts primarily for the global income convergence and rapidly declining poverty rates. Latin America, the Middle East and North Africa showed slower but steady progress in poverty reduction. However, their more modest growth experience implies a relative income deterioration vis-a-vis the richer regions and also East and South Asia, and thus, can be seen as a remaining divergent factor in the global income distribution. Lastly, Sub-Saharan Africa has remained virtually stagnant and has become the poorest region in relative and absolute terms, implying a steady divergence and disconnection from the global growth process. Given the large share of extremely poor people and high poverty headcounts in Sub-Saharan Africa, it is clear from the analysis that any further large gains in extreme poverty reduction can be only achieved by pro-poor, or at least distributionally neutral, growth in Sub-Saharan Africa.

Essay 4: EU-ACP Economic Partnership Agreements

The European Union (EU) and African, Caribbean, and Pacific (ACP) countries have a rather long common history. Due to these special historic relationships, the EU granted more-or-less duty and quota-free access for exports from ACP countries to EU markets. Other developing countries did not receive the same treatment. However, WTO rules only allow different treatment for different types of countries, i.e., it is possible to give preferential access to all developing countries while discriminating against high-income countries. In contrast, it is not possible to give preferential access to some developing countries while discriminating against other developing countries. Thus, the special treatment for ACP countries was not compatible with fundamental WTO principles. However, acknowledging the special relationship between the EU and ACP countries, the EU benefited from a WTO waiver until 2007.

Trade agreements on a reciprocal basis created the possibility of sustaining preferential market access to the EU for ACP countries. Hence, the EU started negotiations focused upon so-called Economic Partnership Agreements (EPAs) with six ACP regions which were self-defined by the ACP countries in 2003. These regions include the Caribbean (CARIFORUM), Central Africa (CEMAC), South-East Africa (ESA), West Africa (ECOWAS), Southern Africa (SADC), and the Pacific.

At the core of the EPAs are regional trade agreements between the EU and each of the six regions of ACP countries. However, the EPAs are also intended to support ACP regional integration, to foster their integration into world markets, and to improve coherence between trade and development. While the previous trade preferences for ACP countries were determined unilaterally by the EU, the current EPAs are jointly designed in negotiations between the EU and the ACP countries. ACP countries are requested to open their markets to EU products to some extent in return for their access to EU markets. However, it is possible that developing countries will open their markets to a much smaller extent than the EU does (in case of the EPAs, an average 80-percent increase in accessibility within 15 years).

Critics claim that EPAs are harmful for ACP countries mainly because the reciprocal market access for EU exports to ACP countries dramatically reduces tariff revenues in ACP countries. Moreover, local industries suffer from stiff competition with companies from the EU. One could argue against such critiques that there is no reasonable alternative to EPAs because the consequence of not having a trade agreement would be the loss of preferential access to EU markets (which would be severe). Nevertheless, the points mentioned by these critiques could be perhaps justified as the price ACP countries have to pay for sustained access to EU markets. Therefore, it is important to estimate the welfare effects of tariff reductions for products from the EU in ACP countries (e.g., the price ACP countries have to pay for sustained access to EU markets). This is done in the fourth essay using as examples nine African countries: Botswana, Cameroon, Côte d'Ivoire, Ghana, Kenya, Mozambique, Namibia, Tanzania, and Uganda.

Studies by Karingi et al. (2005), Milner et al. (2006), Busse and Großmann (2007), and Fontagné et al. (2008) take a similar approach. The main limitations of these previous studies are that elasticities of import demand were chosen rather arbitrarily and, in some cases, that ,only rather general scenarios of tariff reduction are simulated. This essay overcomes these limitations. First, the elasticities of import demand for the nine African countries are estimated from highly disaggregated trade data. Second, the real negotiated tariff reduction rates are applied to access the trade agreement's real welfare effects on the African countries.

The results show that Côte d'Ivoire, Ghana, Kenya, Tanzania, and Uganda experience small welfare losses, while Botswana, Cameroon, Mozambique, and Namibia experience remarkable welfare gains. A simulation comparing the EPA tariff reductions to the theoretical scenario of a full liberalization show that Tanzania and Uganda could also have experienced welfare gains. This indicates that different priorities were in place when excluding certain products from liberalization. Although consumption and trade-creation effects compensate or even overcompensate in most cases for the decline in tariff revenues and appropriate transition periods are in place, the question of revenues remains of importance for the national budget of the African countries (since all of them highly depend upon tariff revenues and because trade with the EU was previously an important source of such revenue). A possible solution to this problem of revenue losses would be for the EU to provide budget support to the most affected countries, to help improve tax administration, and to ensure reliable tax collection. The essay also provides policy conclusions for a number of other questions.

Essay 5: Political Institutions and Human Development

Sen (1983), among others, revolutionized the way economists look at development. Thanks to him, development today is a rather broad concept, whereas economic development oftentimes used to be only a synonym for economic growth. Development, as a whole, depends upon each individual's capabilities, which define the freedoms to choose a valuable life in accordance with individual preferences. This approach inspired the emergence of the pluralist and integrative conception of "human development" and operationalization in the form of the United Nations Development Programme (UNDP) Human Development Index. It is not only income but also health, education, and other factors that enable people to shape their lives in accordance with their desires.

It is the purpose of this fifth essay to answer the question as to which political system is the best for obtaining a high level of human development for the population. Singapore's former president, Lee Kuan Yew, claimed that authoritarian rule is more efficient than democratic governments and therefore beneficial to economic development (and as a consequence, also for human development). There are in fact many examples that could help to prove him right: His own country, Singapore, is today a high income country with life expectancy at birth of 79 years and a literacy rate of 97 percent. Also, the relatively poor Cuba managed to achieve a very high life expectancy rate at birth of 77 years and a literacy rate of 93 percent. The democracy Niger, in contrast, is not only much poorer (the average GDP per capita is eight times higher in Cuba and 32 times higher in Singapore) but also the life expectancy rate is very low at 44 years and only 18 percent of the population is literate. A similar picture holds true for India with a life expectancy rate at birth of 63 years and a literacy rate of 60 percent.

These examples and also controversies in the theoretical literature show that it is not self-evident that democratic governments are superior to autocratic leaders in terms of economic and human development outcomes. The literature points to a possible trade-off between growth-enhancing property rights protection and redistribution. On the one hand, property rights protection is a necessary condition for an increase in the overall wealth of a nation (Acemoglu et al. 2001, 2002), but whether all can benefit depends on redistribution, as well. Moreover, corporatism may lead to lock-in effects and decreasing reform capacity in democracies. The causal direction is not clear: Is democracy a cause or a consequence of the development process? Finally, there is a debate as to which conditions are necessary for democracy to have a positive effect on human development.

Empirical studies with a focus on democracy and economic growth do not provide a coherent answer. Barro (1996), Tavares and Wacziarg (2001), and Minier (1998) find a moderately negative or nonlinear correlation between democracy and growth. In contrast, Persson and Tabellini (2006) and Rodrik and Wacziarg (2005) find a positive, or at least the absence of a negative, correlation between democracy and economic growth. There is also uncertainty about the correlation with democracy for the non-income dimensions of human development. Very few empirical studies focusing on the non-income dimensions of human development and democracy are available. Besley and Kudamatsu (2006) and Tsai (2006) find a positive correlation between democracy and human development, while Ross (2006) finds the opposite. All studies have certain limitations which might explain why they do not have a coherent theme. They are either confined to a sub-sample of developing countries, are focused upon only one dimension of human development, or are restricted to a cross-section which disregards the time dimension of the data. None of the previous empirical studies investigate possible conditions that might have an impact on democracy's performance measured in human development outcomes.

This essay analyzes the relationship between democracy and the non-income dimensions of human development. It extends the existing literature in several ways. The essay develops a theoretical argument as to why democracy should lead to better non-income human development outcomes than authoritarian rule. Capital redistribution is less important for obtaining high levels of GDP per capita in a democracy; for instance, a society with a small group of extremely rich and many poor people could have the same GDP per capita as a society where everybody is moderately rich. However, this is not true for life expectancy or literacy. The life expectancy of a society where a small group reaches age 100 and everyone else dies at age 20 will be very close to 20 years. This is even more obvious for the literacy rate, being a direct measurement of the percentage of the public that reads. Thus, the theoretical reasoning of the essay rests upon the redistributive effects of democracy, based upon qualitative arguments by Sen (1999), among others, and a quantitative argument based on the median voter theory. The empirical section is a panel analysis that covers all countries of the world (subject to data availability) and a time span of 30 years. Moreover, interaction effects are included, as well, to determine whether the performance of democracy is affected by certain circumstances.

The empirical investigation shows a strong and robust correlation between democracy and human development, measured by life expectancy and literacy, and controlling for the level of economic development and other important variables. The model is constructed in such a way, that the correlation can be cautiously interpreted as causal. Interestingly, the interaction between democracy and its presumed conditions of functioning turned out to be insignificant or not robust.

Essay 1

A Likelihood Ratio Test for Bimodality in Two-Component Mixtures

1.1 Introduction

Analyzing the modality of the distribution of a random sample is an important problem, especially for proper graphical visualization of the data. In particular, it is relevant to decide whether modes which are present in a certain fit are merely sampling artifacts or whether they are actual features of the underlying density.

Most testing procedures for multimodality, which were suggested in the literature, are nonparametric in nature. The arguably most popular method, which is based on kernel estimates with the normal kernel, was suggested by Silverman (1981). He observed that for fixed observations the number of modes in such an estimate is a monotonically decreasing function of the bandwidth. Using this fact Silverman (1981) defined the k-critical bandwidth h_k as the minimal bandwidth for which the kernel estimate still just has k modes. If h_k exceeds a critical value, which is constructed from a bootstrap procedure, then the hypothesis for k modes of the underlying density is rejected. See also Mammen et al. (1992), Fisher et al. (1994) and Hall and York (2001). A test for unimodality against multimodality, which is based on measuring the distance between the empirical distribution function and the class of unimodal distribution functions, was introduced by Hartigan and Hartigan (1985), it is called the dip test. Müller and Sawitzki (1991) used the so-called excess mass functional to construct a test for k-modality. For $k = 1$ their test is equivalent to the dip test. See also Fisher and Marron (2001).

The notion of multimodality of the distribution of a population is closely related to the notion of population heterogeneity. A popular way to model population heterogeneity parametrically is via mixture models. In particular, the likelihood ratio test for homogeneity in two-component mixtures has been extensively studied in recent years, cf. e.g. Chen et al. (2001). However, mixtures with two distinct components need not be bimodal, and two component mixtures of

---

based on joint work with Hajo Holzmann.

unimodal component densities can have more than two modes. Therefore, there is no immediate connection between the number of components in a mixture and the number of modes of the resulting density. Nevertheless, the modal structure of two-component mixtures of certain parametric families, notably the normal distribution (Robertson and Fryer, 1969) and the von Mises distribution (Mardia and Sutton, 1975), is completely known in terms of the parameters of the mixture. For two-component mixtures, for which such an explicit characterization of the modal structure is available, we construct a likelihood ratio (LR) test for unimodality against bimodality. The asymptotic distribution of the LR test for bimodality, though not a standard χ^2-distribution, can be deduced from existing results on the behavior of LR statistics on the boundary of the parameter space, cf. Chernoff (1954) and Self and Liang (1987).
When compared to the nonparametric methods mentioned above, the LR test has certain merits as well as certain limitations. Concerning the advantages, the LR test is more powerful than competing nonparametric methods if the distributional assumptions are satisfied. Further, using von Mises mixtures, the LR test can easily be applied to circular data. Note that for circular data, only few methods are available, notably the tests by Fisher and Marron (2001) and by Basu and Jammalamadaka (2002). Moreover, using recent results by Ray and Lindsay (2005) on the modal structure of multivariate normal mixtures, it can be extended to the multivariate setting where no methods seem to be available yet. Concerning limitations, the LR test can only test for unimodality against bimodality and not for k against more than k modes, since there are no parametric descriptions for these cases. Further, it loses power if the mixture component densities are not normally distributed but have heavier tails (like the t-distribution).
Section 1.2 describes the asymptotic distribution of the LR test for bimodality in two-component mixtures and gives two examples. In Section 1.3 we investigate the performance of the LR test via a simulation study. As an application, in Section 1.4, following Pittau (2005) and Pittau and Zelli (2006) we analyze the cross-sectional distribution of per capita log GDP across EU regions via mixtures. After excluding the mere urban areas, it turns out that a two-component mixture model with equal variances for the two components adequately describes the data for all years. We further investigate whether the distribution is actually bimodal, both by using Silverman's test as well as via the LR test for bimodality. Silverman's test can never reject the hypothesis of unimodality. In contrast, for the years 1977-79 the LRT rejects unimodality with level 5%, while in the following years, it can no longer reject this hypothesis with increasing p-values. Thus, while the cross-sectional distribution of per capita log GDP in the EU regions under investigation remains heterogeneous in the sense of being well-modeled by a two-component mixture of normal distributions, these components only significantly result in a bimodal distribution in the years 1977-1979, while in the following years the two components start to merge and form a unimodal distribution.

1.2 The Likelihood Ratio Test for Bimodality

Let $f(x;\theta)$, $\theta \in \Theta \subset \mathbb{R}^d$, $x \in \mathbb{R}^q$, be a parametric family of q-dimensional densities, and consider the two component mixture family

$$f(x;\theta_1,\theta_2,p) = pf(x;\theta_1) + (1-p)f(x;\theta_2),$$

where

$$(\theta_1, \theta_2, p) \in \Theta \times \Theta \times [0,1] = \Theta_{mix} \subset \mathbb{R}^{2d+1}.$$

In order to allow for possible joint parameters of the component densities (e.g. equal variances), we consider a subset $E_{mix} \subset \Theta_{mix}$, where $E_{mix} \subset \mathbb{R}^q$ for a minimal $q \leq 2d+1$. Suppose that the mixture density is at most bimodal, so that we can split the set E_{mix} disjointly into $E_{mix} = E_{unim} \cup E_{bim}$, the unimodal part E_{unim} and the bimodal part E_{bim}. We will denote the boundary between E_{bim} and E_{unim} by ∂E_{unim}, i.e. $\partial E_{unim} = E_{unim} \cap \overline{E_{bim}}$, where $\overline{E_{bim}}$ denotes the closure of E_{bim}. Given observations $X_1, \ldots, X_n$ from the mixture density, we consider the log-likelihood function

$$\mathscr{L}_n(\theta_1, \theta_2, p) = \sum_{k=1}^{n} \log f(X_k; \theta_1, \theta_2, p).$$

Assumption 1. The partial derivatives of $\log f(x; \theta_1, \theta_2, p)$ of order 3 with respect to θ_1, θ_2 and p exist a.s., at least in a neighborhood N of the true value $(\theta_1^0, \theta_2^0, p^0)$.

Assumption 2. For $(\theta_1, \theta_2, p) \in N$, the first and second order partial derivatives of $f(x; \theta_1, \theta_2, p)$ are uniformly bounded in absolute value by a function $F(x) \in L_1(\mathbb{R})$, and the third order partial derivatives of $\log f(x; \theta_1, \theta_2, p)$ are uniformly bounded in absolute value by a function $H(x)$ with $EH(X_1) < \infty$.

Assumption 3. The expectation of the matrix of second order partial derivatives of $\log f(x; \theta_1, \theta_2, p)$ is finite and positive definite for $(\theta_1, \theta_2, p) \in N$.

Note that Assumption 3 will not be satisfied in a neighborhood of a single component density (i.e. if $p = 0$ or $p = 1$ or $\theta_1 = \theta_2$, see e.g. Goffinet et al., 1992). However, for unimodal component densities such as normal or von Mises densities (see the examples below), a density on the boundary ∂E_{unim} will be a proper two-component mixture, so that Assumption 3 is satisfied.

Theorem 1. *Suppose that the true parameter vector $(\theta_1^0, \theta_2^0, p^0)$ of the mixture density lies on the boundary ∂E_{unim}, and that locally around $(\theta_1^0, \theta_2^0, p^0)$, ∂E_{unim} is a smooth $(q-1)$-dimensional surface in $\mathbb{R}^q$. If furthermore Assumptions 1 - 3 hold true, then we have that*

$$R_n := 2\Big(\sup_{(\theta_1,\theta_2,p)\in E_{mix}} \mathscr{L}_n(\theta_1, \theta_2, p) - \sup_{(\theta_1,\theta_2,p)\in E_{unim}} \mathscr{L}_n(\theta_1, \theta_2, p)\Big) \xrightarrow{\mathscr{D}} (\chi_0^2 + \chi_1^2)/2, \qquad (1.1)$$

where χ_0^2 is the measure with mass one at $x = 0$ and χ_1^2 is the chi-square distribution with 1 degree of freedom.

This result follows from the theory of the likelihood ratio test for parameter vectors which lie on the boundary of the parameter space, cf. Chernoff (1954) and Self and Liang (1987). Note that if the true parameter vector lies in the interior of E_{unim}, then due to consistency, the unrestricted maximum likelihood estimator will asymptotically lie in a neighborhood U of θ_0 with $U \subset E_{unim}$, so that $R_n \to 0$ in probability. Therefore the test will also asymptotically keep the level in this case.

Example 1 (*Normal distribution).* For the normal density $f(x;\mu,\sigma)=\frac{1}{\sqrt{2\pi}\sigma}e^{\left(-\frac{(x-\mu)^2}{2\sigma^2}\right)}$ we obtain the general two component mixture as follows:

$$f(x;p,\mu_1,\mu_2,\sigma_1,\sigma_2)=pf(x;\mu_1,\sigma_1)+(1-p)f(x;\mu_2,\sigma_2), \tag{1.2}$$

where $0\leq p\leq 1$ and without loss of generality, $\mu_2\geq\mu_1$. Introducing the parameters $r=\sigma_1/\sigma_2$ and $d=(\mu_2-\mu_1)/(2\sqrt{\sigma_1\sigma_2})$, one easily sees that $f(x;p,\mu_1,\mu_2,\sigma_1,\sigma_2)$ has the same number of modes as $f(x;p,-d,d,r,1/r)$, cf. Behboodian (1970). Thus, bimodality solely depends on the three parameters (p,d,r). Let us mention that such an argument can be made for general location-scale families (e.g. also for the t-distribution with fixed degrees of freedom). In case of equal variances, $\sigma_1=\sigma_2=\sigma$, one obtains $r=1$, and the conditions read as follows: $f(x;p,\mu_1,\mu_2,\sigma)$ is unimodal if and only if $d\leq 1$ or if

$$d>1 \quad \text{and} \quad |\log(1-p)-\log p|\geq 2\log(d-\sqrt{d^2-1})+2d\sqrt{d^2-1}, \tag{1.3}$$

otherwise, it is bimodal. In Figure 1.1, the region of bimodality is depicted, where for $r\neq 1$ the characterization in Robertson and Fryer (1969) was used.

If we assume that the variances $\sigma_1=\sigma_2=\sigma$ are equal (though possibly unknown) and that p is known and fixed, then the smoothness assumption on the boundary of the unimodal parameter domain is satisfied everywhere, and thus Theorem 1 holds true.

This is e.g. obvious for the case $p=1/2$, in which case the mixture is unimodal with mode at $(\mu_1+\mu_2)/2$ if and only if $\mu_2-\mu_1\leq 2\sigma$. For other values of p it follows from equation (1.3). However, in case of variable p and equal variances, the boundary has a singularity for $d=1$ and $p=1/2$, which follows from equation (1.3) by taking equality there and the limit $d\to 1$.
If $d=1$ and $p=1/2$, the likelihood ratio statistic will be asymptotically stochastically smaller than the limit distribution in (1.1). This is because the angle between the tangents to the bimodal region at these points is less than π, so that the unrestricted ML estimator will in more than 50% of all cases fall into the unimodal region, and the LR statistic will be zero. See also Figure 1.1. In summary, a test based on the critical value of the $1/2(\chi_0^2+\chi_1^2)$ distribution will asymptotically keep the level everywhere in the unimodal parameter space. Extensions to the characterization of the number of modes of higher dimensional normal distributions were recently obtained by Ray and Lindsay (2005).

Example 2 (*Von Mises distribution).* The von Mises distribution is given by the density

$$f(x;\mu,\kappa)=\frac{1}{2\pi I_0(\kappa)}\exp\left(\kappa\cos(x-\mu)\right), \qquad 0\leq x<2\pi,$$

where $\mu\in[0,2\pi)$, $\kappa>0$ and $I_0(\kappa)$ is a norming factor given by the modified Bessel function of the second kind. The two component mixture of von Mises distributions will be denoted by

$$f(x;p,\mu_1,\mu_2,\kappa_1,\kappa_2)=pf(x;\mu_1,\kappa_1)+(1-p)f(x;\mu_2,\kappa_2),$$

where w.l.o.g. $\mu_2-\mu_1=:d\in[0,\pi]$ (since the maximal distance on the circle of two points along the arc is π). Mardia and Sutton (1975) give precise conditions for bimodality for general parameters constellations. Here we only review their results for the case of equal concentration parameters, i.e. $\kappa_1=\kappa_2=\kappa$. In this case, the mixture is unimodal if and only if either $d=0$ or

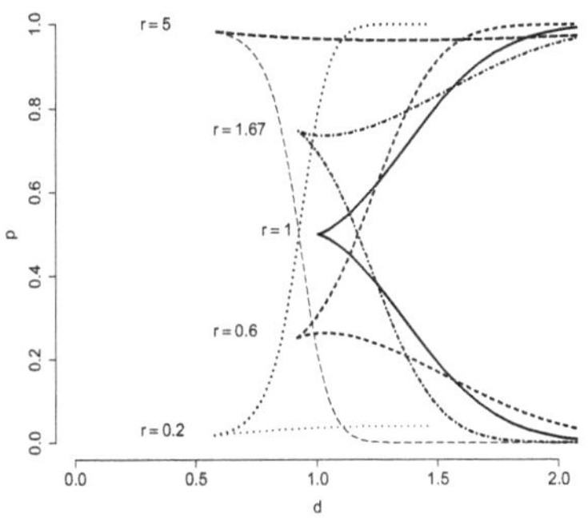

Figure 1.1: Regions of bimodality of the normal distribution, where $d = (\mu_2 - \mu_1)/(2\sqrt{\sigma_1\sigma_2})$ and $r = \sigma_1/\sigma_2$. On the right side of the curves are those parameter constellations of p and d for which for fixed r the resulting mixture is bimodal.

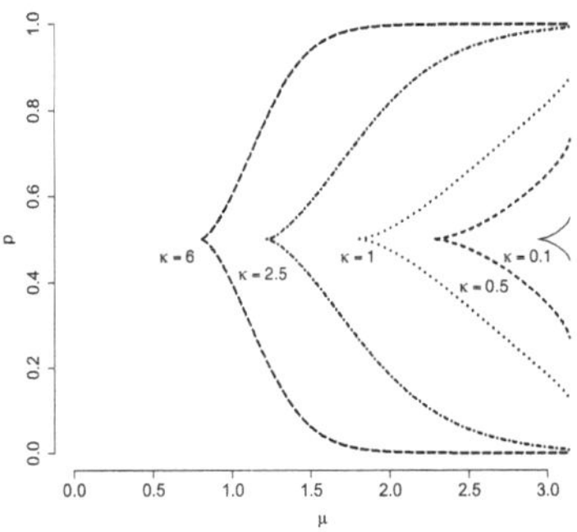

Figure 1.2: Regions of bimodality of the von Mises distribution, where $\mu = \mu_2 - \mu_1$ and $\kappa_1 = \kappa_2 = \kappa$. On the right side of the curves are those parameter constellations of p and μ for which for fixed κ the resulting mixture is bimodal.

- $d = \pi$ and $0 \leq p \leq (1+\exp(2\kappa))^{-1}$ or $(1+\exp(-2\kappa))^{-1} \leq p \leq 1$ or
- $0 < d < \pi$ and either
  - $\sin d < 2\kappa \sin^3(d/2)$, $\quad 0 \leq p \leq 1$, $\quad$ or
  - $\sin d \geq 2\kappa \sin^3(d/2)$ and $0 \leq p \leq -t(\delta)/(1-t(\delta))$ or $1/(1-t(\delta)) \leq p \leq 1$, where δ is the solution of

$$2\kappa\cos^3\delta - \kappa(1+\cos d)\cos\delta - 2\cos(d/2) = 0, \qquad 0 < \delta < d/2, \tag{1.4}$$

and

$$t(\delta) = -\frac{\sin(d/2+\delta)}{\sin(d/2-\delta)}\exp\big(-2\kappa\sin(d/2)\sin\delta\big).$$

The conditions for von Mises mixtures are more complicated than those for normal mixtures, since it is not a simple location-scale family (this notion is not defined for circular distributions). Still, although one has to distinguish several cases, these cases merge continuously. For example, for $\sin d = 2\kappa\sin^3(d/2)$, the mixture is still unimodal for all $0 \leq p \leq 1$. Further, for $d \to \pi$, one has that $-t(\delta)/(1-t(\delta)) \to (1+\exp(2\kappa))^{-1}$ (and similarly on the other side). In Figure 1.2, the region of bimodality is displayed.

For fixed p, Theorem 1 is again generally applicable. However, for p variable and equal concentration parameters, there occurs a singularity on the boundary of the set of unimodal parameter constellations for $p = 0.5$ if $\sin d = 2\kappa \sin^3(d/2)$. Again, the test will nevertheless asymptotically keep the critical value.

1.3 Simulations

In this section we conduct a simulation study in order to analyze the practical feasibility of the LR test for bimodality.
First let us investigate the quality of the approximation by the asymptotic distribution as given in Theorem 1. To this end, for certain parameter constellations on the boundary of the unimodal region we simulate the actual level of the test when using asymptotic critical values. Here we use 10^4 samples of various sizes. Further, direct numerical maximization of the log-likelihood function is employed, and for the constrained estimate we reparameterize the problem in order to use unconstrained maximization.

Table 1.1: Simulated level of R_n on the boundary for normal mixtures, using asymptotic critical values

scenario	free parameters	sample size	nominal level	simulated level
$\mu_1 = 0,\ \mu_2 = 3$	μ_1, μ_2, p	100	0.10	0.12
$\sigma_1 = \sigma_2 = \sigma = 1.3$			0.05	0.059
$p = 0.442$			0.01	0.015
		250	0.10	0.11
			0.05	0.057
			0.01	0.012
	μ_1, μ_2, p, σ	250	0.10	0.14
			0.05	0.072
			0.01	0.016
		500	0.10	0.13
			0.05	0.066
			0.01	0.014
$\mu_1 = 0,\ \mu_2 = 2.5$	μ_1, μ_2, p	100	0.10	0.16
$\sigma_1 = 1.1,\ \sigma_2 = 0.8$			0.05	0.086
			0.01	0.019
		250	0.10	0.10
			0.05	0.052
			0.01	0.011

The results for the normal distribution are displayed in Table 1.1, simulations for the von Mises distribution led to similar results. It turns out that the test keeps the nominal level quite well even for moderate sample sizes, both for normal and von Mises mixtures, as long as either equal variances (or concentration parameters) are employed or if the variances are assumed to be known. However, further simulations indicated that if both variances are allowed to vary, the approximation is rather inaccurate and should not be used.

Now let us investigate the power properties of the LR test for bimodality. For simplicity we restrict ourselves to normal mixtures, and we compare the performance with Silverman's (1981) test and with the Dip test by Hartigan and Hartigan (1985). When implementing Silverman's (1981) test we use 1000 bootstrap replications to estimate the critical value for the bandwidth. Further the R-library "Diptest" is used for the Dip test by Hartigan and Hartigan (1985). We consider several alternative scenarios. In each scenario 1000 samples of various sizes are generated.

a. First alternative: a normal mixture $f_1(x) = f(x, 0.5, -1.5, 1.5, 1, 1)$. The density is symmetric and clearly bimodal, cf. Figure A.1. where also the unrestricted ML fit and the ML fit restricted to the unimodal region are displayed for a sample from f_1. Here we use only equal variances, and σ is allowed to vary. The LR test performs slightly superior to Silverman's test, and both outperform the Dip test. See Table 1.2 for the simulation results.

Table 1.2: Power under first alternative, the normal mixture $f_1 = f(x, 0.5, -1.5, 1.5, 1, 1)$

sample size	nominal level	LR	Silverman's	Dip
200	0.10	0.89	0.77	0.30
	0.05	0.80	0.63	0.20
	0.01	0.53	0.35	0.06
500	0.10	0.99	0.97	0.60
	0.05	0.98	0.92	0.47
	0.01	0.93	0.75	0.24

b. Second alternative: a normal mixture $f_2(x) = f(x, 0.3, -1.5, 1, 0.75, 0.75)$. The density is asymmetric but bimodal, cf. Figure A.2. Again we only use equal variances for the fit, and σ is allowed to vary. The results are displayed in Table 1.3. The dip test has no significant power exceeding the level for this hypothesis for sample sizes up to $n = 500$, and the LR test strongly outperforms Silverman's test.

Table 1.3: Power under second alternative, the normal mixture $f_2 = f(x, 0.3, -1.5, 1, 0.75, 0.75)$

sample size	nominal level	LR	Silverman's
200	0.10	0.80	0.57
	0.05	0.70	0.39
	0.01	0.45	0.11
500	0.10	0.99	0.97
	0.05	0.98	0.92
	0.01	0.93	0.75

c. Third alternative: a normal mixture $f_3(x) = f(x, 0.6, -1.5, 1.4, 0.6, 1.4)$. The density is asymmetric but bimodal, cf. Figure A.2. Here we use distinct variances which are assumed to be known. Only the LR test has a reasonable power against this alternative, and therefore we do not present a table for this simulation setting. In fact, the comparison is not really fair since the LR test uses the exact values of the variances, which are hardly available in practice.
d. We also investigated the behavior of the LR test for bimodality if the distributional assumption of normal mixtures is not satisfied, and briefly report the results. We simulated 1000 samples of sizes 200 and 500 from a mixture of two t-distributions with 5 degrees of freedom. One component has location parameter 0 and the other 3. Both have unit scaling parameter, and a weight of $p = 0.4$ for the first component is used. The density is clearly bimodal. However, due to the heavy tails of the t-distribution, the variance in the normal fit is typically too large. Therefore the modes in the normal mixture are much less distinctive than in the t mixture, and the LR test looses power. In fact, the LR test looses much power as compared to Silverman's test, while the LR test and the dip test perform similarly.

1.4 Application to the Cross-Regional Income Distribution in the EU

The convergence hypothesis states that poorer economies are growing faster than richer ones, hence, catching up such that eventually there will be no differences between real average per capita income across countries. This would imply a unimodal cross-national or even cross-regional distribution of income which should become constantly less dispersed. The literature distinguishes between two types of convergence, β-convergence and σ-convergence (Sala-i-Martin, 1996). By definition, β-convergence occurs if the coefficient on initial income is negative when regressed on the change of log real income, or in words, if initially poorer economies grow on average faster than the initially rich. Moreover, σ-convergence is defined as the decrease of the dispersion of the entire income distribution measured by the standard deviation of log incomes. If there are no other control variables in the growth regression, we speak of absolute β-convergence, which would be a necessary but not a sufficient condition for σ-convergence. Thus, for the convergence hypothesis to hold we need absolute ß-convergence and σ-convergence such that the income distribution converges to one common mode.
However, the extended Solow growth model, given its assumptions, only implies a restricted type of conditional β-convergence. Indeed, if two groups of countries are governed by different parameters, but display within group homogeneity of parameters, it would imply a divergence of the two groups, but a within group convergence of economies to their respective group steady state. Quah (1997) developed a theoretical and empirical framework for so called club convergence from the viewpoint of income distribution dynamics, implying an emerging twin peaks phenomenon for the global cross-country income distribution. Bianchi (1997) finds empirical evidence for a bimodal cross-country income distribution occurring in the 1970s for all subsequent years. For regions in the European Union this picture however is less clear (cf. e.g. Quah, 1996c, and Le Gallo, 2004).

The framework of EU regions is of special interest, since cohesion among EU regions has been a major priority of all EU treaties so far. The European Development Fund (EDF) has been in operation since the very beginning in 1959. Starting with 3.4 million Euro, it went up to 244.7 million Euro in 1977 and 1353.6 million Euro in 1993. Other relevant policy outcomes are the European Agricultural Guidance and Guarantee Fund (EAGGF) established in 1962 and the European Regional Development Fund (ERDF) created in 1975. The EAGGF started with 28.7 million Euro in 1975, increasing to 6587.1 million Euro in 1977 and 34935.8 million Euro in 1993. The EDF already started with 150 million Euro and increased to 400 million Euro in 1977 and 5382.6 million Euro in 1993.[1] Hence, one should expect that policy interventions assimilate the parameters of the extended Solow growth model in the European Union over time, implying absolute convergence in the long-run. Furthermore, Barro and Sala-i-Martin (1991) argue that convergence of incomes between regions is in general supported and accelerated by an economic environment without restrictions on the free movement of capital, labor and tradeable goods, which is the case in the European Union.

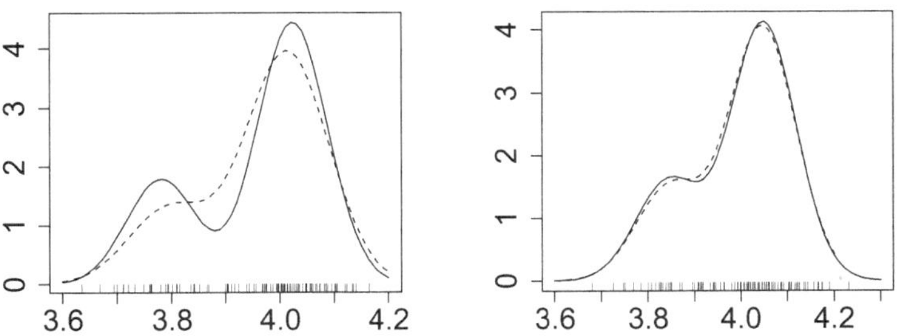

Figure 1.3: Unrestricted (solid lines) and restricted unimodal (dashed lines) fits to the cross-sectional distribution of log GDP PPS per capita for European regions in the years 1977 (left) and 1993 (right).

We use a data set on regional GDP in the European Union available from CRENoS [2], covering the period from 1977 to 1993 and including administrative regions defined by the Nomenclature of the Territorial Units for Statistics (NUTS) established by Eurostat. The GDP figures are given in 1990 constant prices and are converted to Purchasing Power Standard (PPS). The data set includes regions from all EU-12 member countries at that time. Following Pittau (2005) and Pittau and Zelli (2006) we use the territorial units as follows: NUTS-0 (countries) for Denmark, Luxembourg and Ireland; NUTS-1 for Belgium (3 Régions), West-Germany (11 Länder), the Netherlands (4 Landsdelen) and UK (9 Government Office Regions and 3 Countries); NUTS-2

[1]For these facts see: European Commission (2000), The Community Budget: The Facts in Figures.

[2]Center for North South Economic Research, http://www.crenos.it

for Italy (20 Regioni), France (22 Régions), Spain (17 Communitades Autonomas), Portugal (5 Comissaoes de Coordenacao Regional), Greece (13 Development Regions). Though not equally sized, these regions are, due to administrative structure of the different countries, the best units available for comparisons below the national level. Urban regions usually have their own economic structure and are not comparable to regions covering both urban and rural parts. Therefore we decided to exclude the mainly urban regions from our analysis (Brüssel B3, Bremen D4, Hamburg D5, Ile de France F1 and Luxembourg LU).

Pittau (2005) and Pittau and Zelli (2006) analyze a similar data set (without the exclusion of the urban regions) by using finite mixtures of normal distributions. For our more homogeneous data set, in a first step we determine the number of components in the mixture as well as the structure of the mixture (in particular equal or unequal variances for the components of the mixture). To this end we use the model selection criteria AIC and BIC. Table B.1 shows the results for the years 1977 and 1990. Both model selection criteria select the two-component mixture model with equal variances for the components. This is in fact true for all years from 1977-1993, thus, it is the model of choice for this period.

Pittau (2005) and Pittau and Zelli (2006) also test the number of components by using a bootstrap version of the likelihood ratio test. Here, in order to confirm that two components are indeed present in the data, we use the modified likelihood ratio test for homogeneity (cf. Chen et al., 2001). In contrast to the usual LRT for homogeneity, this test retains a comparatively simple limit theory, thus a parametric bootstrap (with the resulting loss in power) is not necessary. We test the hypothesis of a single normal distribution against a two-component mixture with equal (but unkown) variance, and to this end use a version of the modified LRT with a structural parameter as investigated in Chen and Kalbfleisch (2005). They show that the χ^2_2-distribution is an asymptotic upper bound for the distribution of the modified LRT statistic in this case. Based on this bound we find p-values of less than 0.001 for all years in the period 1977-1993, thus, there is strong statistical evidence of two components in the distribution.

Nevertheless, as discussed in the introduction this does not necessarily imply that the distribution is bimodal, so that the components are strongly pronounced. Therefore, we test for unimodality against bimodality, both by using the LRT for bimodality in a two-component normal mixture

Table 1.4: Tests for unimodality for the distribution of log GDP per capita in European regions

year	p-val LRT	p-val. Silverman
1977	0.006	0.14
1978	0.009	0.23
1979	0.042	0.29
1980	0.105	0.28
1985	0.222	0.98
1990	0.214	0.69
1993	0.347	0.54

with equal variances, as well as using Silverman's test. The results are displayed in Table 1.4. While Silverman's test never rejects the hypothesis of a single mode, the LRT rejects in favor of bimodality in 1977–1979. Afterward, the hypothesis can no longer be rejected, indicating that the two groups, though still present, start to merge. Figure 1.3 shows the restricted unimodal and the unrestricted fit for the years 1977 and 1993, respectively.

Conclusions can be drawn both from an economical and a statistical point of view. Economically the empirical results indicate that the two component mixture describing the cross-regional income distribution in the European Union became less and less dispersed, meaning that well separated clusters of poor and rich regions in the EU moved closer together and might tend to converge to a single group in the long-run. However, further research is necessary to evaluate the long-run impact of EU cohesion policy on regional GDP, of special interest would be an analysis of the distribution dynamics past the more recent EU enlargements. From a statistical point of view, we find, that the LRT is able to detect a second mode in a real-data application, while Silverman´s test is not able to do so.

Essay 2

Twin Peaks or Three Components?

2.1 Introduction

The behavior of the cross-national income distribution is for many reasons of great interest. In particular, the development of twin or even more peaks would characterize a world of growing cross-country average income polarization and suggest the existence of multiple equilibria. Numerous papers (Barro, 1991; Barro and Sala-i-Martin, 1992; Levine and Renelt, 1992; Mankiw et al., 1992; Jones, 1997; Quah, 1996a,b, 1997; Romer, 1990; Sala-i-Martin, 1996; Durlauf et al., 2005; Beaudry et al., 2005; Graham and Temple, 2006) have this debate at heart and discuss, which type of convergence governs the development of the cross-national income distribution and what is to be expected in the future. In particular, they show that a focus on β-convergence is informative on the nature of intra-distributional dynamics but cannot convey information concerning the development of the entire distribution, which appears to be polarizing. In order to overcome this traditional shortcoming of the β-convergence debate, probabilistic income mobility models are used to estimate likelihoods of convergence groups. Hence, there is a discussion on whether the so called twin peak phenomenon is either persistent as probabilities of switching are too low (Quah, 1996a,b) or is only a temporary occurrence due to increasing frequencies of growth miracles (Jones, 1997). Thus, existing literature either shows a descriptive picture of the cross-national income distribution by observing the development of two income per capita peaks in the cross-national income distribution, or, alternatively, is concerned with β-convergence in cross-national income growth regressions. Bianchi (1997) employed a nonparametric test for multimodality based on kernel density estimation to the cross-country income distribution. Further nonparametric approaches include those by Anderson (2004), who used stochastic dominance techniques, and by Maasoumi et al. (2007), who analyzed the cross-sectional distribution of growth rates. Regarding parametric modeling, for the cross-country income distribution, Paap and Dijk (1998) used a two-component mixture, consisting of a truncated normal distribution and a Weibull distribution.

---

based on joint work with Hajo Holzmann and Julian Weisbrod.

From nonparametric kernel density estimates, several authors find a twin-peaked cross-country income distribution (Quah, 1996b; Bianchi, 1997). In particular, Bianchi (1997) observes increasing evidence for bimodality in the GDP per capita distribution across countries over the period from 1970 to 1989, indicating global divergence rather than convergence. However, income data are often analyzed on a logarithmic scale, and the number of modes of the log-income distribution may differ substantially from the number of modes of the income distribution itself. In contrast, when modeling a density as a finite mixture, the number of components of this mixture is independent of the chosen scale. Furthermore, if one wishes to address convergence one can argue that it is not the number of modes in the cross-national income density which contains the most relevant information, but rather the number of convergence clubs, which correspond to the components in the finite mixture.

When modeling the cross-national income distribution by a finite mixture, determining its number of components is an essential step in the analysis. In their model, Paap and Dijk (1998) use a mixture with two distinct components, which resembles the fit of a histogram of the cross-national income distribution. Thus, the "stylized fact" of a distinction between poor and rich countries is already built into their model. We argue that via a statistical inference procedure, the data itself should determine the number of components and to this end a finite mixture with normal components of the log-income distribution (or log-normal components of the income distribution itself) is the appropriate tool. We shall apply the recently developed modified likelihood ratio test methodology (cf. Chen et al. 2001, 2004, and Chen and Kalbfleisch, 2005) for the number of components in a finite mixture to the cross-national income distribution.

In contrast to the twin-peaks literature and also to Paap and Dijk (1998), we find evidence of two components only at the beginnings of the 70s, whereas in the mid 70s, a third intermediate component emerges, which tends to separate itself ever more clearly from the poorest component. Thus, we find statistical evidence for three components rather than "twin peaks" in the cross-country income distribution.

After determining the number of components (three components from 1976 onward), we contribute to the convergence debate by extensively investigating the evolution, number of components and the inter-distributional dynamics of the cross-country income distribution by using the posterior probability estimates from our fitted model. In particular, we find intra-distributional dynamics for Asian (upward mobility) and Latin American (downward mobility) countries. The overall picture that we obtain is that of three diverging groups in the cross-national income distribution.

2.2 Statistical Methodology and Data

2.2.1 Data

Following most other papers, our analysis is based on income data from the Penn World Tables Version 6.2, from which we extract the real PPP GDP per capita series of all years and countries available (chain series, base year 2000 in international $).

In order to compare our observations over time, we restrict ourselves to those countries, of which complete income data for the whole time period are available. Further we decided to exclude small oil states or tax heavens, and for simplicity we therefore excluded countries having less than half a million inhabitants. This restriction leaves 124 countries for the period from 1970 to 2003 in our analysis. These countries represent about 95 percent of the world's population.

2.2.2 Testing for the Number of Components in a Finite Mixture

Let f_X denote the density of the cross-country income distribution of a fixed year, and let f_Y be the corresponding density of the log-incomes, so that $f_Y(y) = f_X(e^y)e^y$. Multimodality of f_X can arise by f_X being a finite mixture of other (unimodal) densities, so that

$$f_X(x) = p_1 g(x;\mu_1,\sigma_1) + \ldots + p_m g(x;\mu_m,\sigma_m), \qquad x > 0, \tag{2.1}$$

where the weights $p_i \geq 0$, $\sum_i p_i = 1$ and $g(x;\mu,\sigma)$ is a parametric family of densities, e.g. the log-normal distribution.
If f_X is a finite mixture of densities $g(\cdot;\mu,\sigma)$, there is no general simple connection between the number of modes of f_X and the number of components m. Typically, for unimodal g, the number of modes of f will be at most m, but often will be less than m. Furthermore, one is rather interested in the number of components m of the finite mixture than in the number of modes. For example, in the cross-country income distribution the components correspond to groups with different income level. Therefore, if we model the cross-country distribution of income by a finite mixture, determining its number of components statistically is a task of major importance, since this number will have essential economic consequences.
Further, the number of components is preserved if the data are transformed via a strictly monotonic transformation. Therefore, in this essay we model f_X (and hence f_Y) as a finite mixture and then determine its number of components, mainly via hypothesis testing, but also by the use of model selection criteria. We model f_Y as a finite mixture of normal distributions, so that f_X is a finite mixture of log-normal distributions.
Estimation in finite mixture models (with a fixed number of components) typically proceeds by maximum likelihood. However, the likelihood function in a finite normal mixture with different variances is unbounded, thus, a global maximizer of the likelihood function does not exist. There are some solutions around this problem. One is to look for the largest local maximum. Another is to bound the variances by restrictions of the form $\sigma_i^2 \leq c\sigma_j^2$ for all $i, j = 1, \ldots m$ and some $c > 1$ (cf. Hathaway 1985), which again leads to the existence of a global maximum and, if the true parameters satisfy the restriction, consistency. These solutions have practical problems, since the unknown true parameter has to fulfill the assumed restrictions, and therefore, here and regarding the analysis in Section 2.3 we shall use finite mixtures with equal variances. For further discussion see Section 2.2.4.
Testing in parametric models is often accomplished by using the likelihood ratio test (LRT). However, in order to test for the number of components in finite mixture models, it has long been known that the standard theory of the LRT does not apply: the asymptotic distribution is the superimum over a truncated Gaussian process (Dacunha-Castelle and Gassiat, 1999), and hence is impractical for applications.

Recently, Chen et al. (2001, 2004) and Chen and Kalbfleisch (2005) suggested modified LRTs to partly overcome these problems, which retain a comparatively simple limit theory as well as the good power properties of the LRT. We shall apply these tests to our problem concerning the number of groups in the income distribution. At this point, we want to mention that the LRT and also the modified LRT are invariant under strictly monotonic transformation of the data (if candidate densities are correspondingly transformed). Thus, we could test on the level of the x_i as well as on the level of the y_i, the results are (in contrast to Silverman's test) completely consistent. For convenience, we shall use the log-data.

We first consider testing one against two components in a mixture. Suppose that $\phi(y;\mu,\sigma)$ is the normal distribution with mean μ and standard deviation σ, and consider the two-component mixture

$$f_Y(y;p,\mu_1,\mu_2,\sigma) = p\phi(y;\mu_1,\sigma) + (1-p)\phi(y;\mu_2,\sigma) \tag{2.2}$$

with equal standard deviation σ. The testing problem is

H_1 : f_Y is normally distributed against K_1 : f_Y is of the form (2.2).

The modified likelihood function is given by

$$l_n(p,\mu_1,\mu_2,\sigma) = \sum_{i=1}^{n} \log\big(p\phi(y_i;\mu_1,\sigma) + (1-p)\phi(y_i;\mu_2,\sigma)\big) + h(p),$$

where $h(p)$ is a penalty function which satisfies $h(1/2) = 0$ and $h(p) \to -\infty$, $p \to 0, 1$. The choice of h is discussed in Chen et al. (2001) and Li et al. (2009), it does not have much effect on the performance of the MLRT. We shall use $h(p) = 2\log\big(p(1-p)\big)$. Let $(\hat{p},\hat{\mu}_1,\hat{\mu}_2,\hat{\sigma})$ maximize $l_n(p,\mu_1,\mu_2,\sigma)$ over the full parameter space, and let $(\hat{\mu},\hat{\sigma})$ maximize $l_n(1/2,\mu,\mu,\sigma)$. The hypothesis H_1 is rejected for large values of the modified LRT statistic

$$M_n = 2\big(l_n(\hat{p},\hat{\mu}_1,\hat{\mu}_2,\hat{\sigma}) - l_n(1/2,\hat{\mu},\hat{\mu},\hat{\sigma})\big).$$

More precisely, Chen et al. (2001) show that for known σ, M_n asymptotically follows the distribution $1/2\chi_0^2 + 1/2\chi_1^2$, where χ_0^2 is the point mass at zero. For unknown σ, as formulated above, the precise asymptotic distribution of M_n is unknown, however, Chen and Kalbfleisch (2005) show that the χ_2^2 distribution is an upper bound to the asymptotic distribution of M_n.

Chen et al. (2004) also consider the problem of testing for two against more components of a mixture distribution. More precisely, the problem is to test

$H_2 : f_Y$ is of the form (2.2) against K_2 : f_Y has more than two components.

Here, we again assume equal variances for all components, also under the alternative. Furthermore, one fixes a maximal number of components under the alternative (which can also be estimated, e.g. $m = 4$). For a mixture with m components, slightly changing the notation, the modified maximum likelihood estimators (MLEs) are defined as the maximizer of

$$l_n(\mu_1,\ldots,\mu_m,\sigma) = \sum_{i=1}^{n} \log\big(p_1\phi(y_1;\mu_1,\sigma) + \ldots + p_m\phi(y_m;\mu_m,\sigma)\big) + C\log\Big(\prod_{i=1}^{m} p_i\Big),$$

where $C > 0$ is some fixed constant (we take $C = 2$, its exact choice does not influence the performance of the test much, see Chen et al., 2004). These estimates are then inserted into the LRT statistic. Chen et al. (2004) showed that given a known σ, this modified LRT is asymptotically distributed as $q\chi_0^2 + \frac{1}{2}\chi_1^2 + (1-q)\chi_2^2$, where the proportion q depends on the mixing distributions. For unknown σ, Chen and Kalbfleisch indicate that the χ_3^2 distribution is an upper bound of the asymptotic distribution.

As an illustration, we give the results of the analysis of the year 1976. The complete results are discussed in Section 2.3.1. First we fit a single normal distribution to the log-income distribution (log to the base 10). Doing so, we obtain the following parameters: $\hat{\mu} = 3.52$ and $\hat{\sigma} = 0.46$. The modified MLEs of the two-component mixture with equal variances are calculated as $\hat{p} = 0.51$, $\hat{\mu}_1 = 3.15$, $\hat{\mu}_2 = 3.89$ and $\hat{\sigma} = 0.26$. The resulting value of the modified likelihood ratio function is equal to $T_n = 14.00$, which based on the upper bound of the χ_2^2-distribution yields a p-value of 0.0009. Thus, the hypothesis of a single component is clearly rejected.

Next we consider testing two against three (or more) components. Concerning the fit using three components and equal variances, the parameter estimates based on penalized maximum likelihood are given by

$$\hat{p}_1 = 0.38, \quad \hat{p}_2 = 0.34, \quad \hat{\mu}_1 = 3.04, \quad \hat{\mu}_2 = 3.58, \quad \hat{\mu}_3 = 4.07, \quad \hat{\sigma} = 0.18. \tag{2.3}$$

The resulting value of the modified LR statistic is $T_n = 7.91$. Based on the upper bound by a χ_3^2-distribution, this gives a p-value of 0.048, in favor of three components. The three-component fit based on the modified MLEs, both for the y_i's as well as for the x_i's, are displayed in Figure 2.1.

Apart from testing the number of components, we also compare the mixture models via two popular model selection criteria, namely the Akaike information criterion (AIC) and the Bayesian information criterion (BIC), given by $-2l + 2k$ and $-2l + k\log n$, respectively, where l is the log-likelihood, k the number of parameters and n the number of observations. The results are displayed in Table B.1.

Here, the model selected by AIC is the model with three components, while BIC is slightly in favor of a model with only two components. Although it is theoretically known that the BIC is consistent in finite mixtures (Kerebin, 2000), in finite samples it often selects too few components.

In Figure B.1 we compare the fitted three-component density with a nonparametric density estimate with bandwidth $h_c(3)$ (cf. Section 2.2.5). Such a comparison could also be used for a formal goodness of fit test for our mixture model, cf. e.g. Fan (1994). The nonparametric and our parametric estimate are quite close, thus, our model of the data seems appropriate. In Figure B.2, we furthermore plot the empirical cumulative distribution function (cdf) of the data and the cdf of the fitted three component mixture, Figure 2.1 comprises a Quantile-Quantile (QQ) plot of the data against the fitted mixture. Both plots clearly show that the three component mixture with equal variances provides an good fit.

The whole picture that we get from our analysis of the log cross-country income distribution in 1976, taking into account the modified likelihood ratio tests and the model selection criteria, the shape of nonparametric density estimates and the QQ plots as well as the plots of the cdfs, shows that the three component mixture with equal variances adequately describes the data.

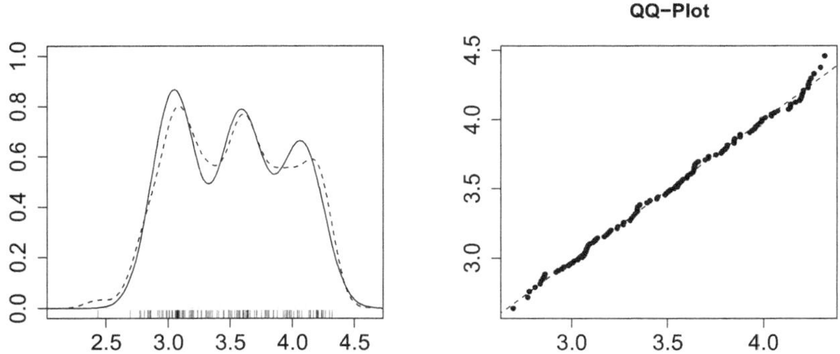

Figure 2.1: Left: Three-component mixture density with equal variances (solid line) and kernel density estimate based on $h_c(3)$ (dashed line) for the log-data (logarithm to the base 10) for 1976. Right: QQ-Plot of the log-data for 1976 against the quantiles of the normal mixture (three components, equal variances) together with least squares fit (dashed line).

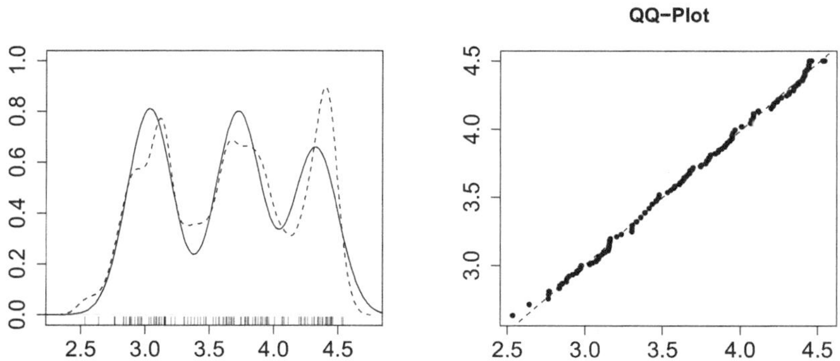

Figure 2.2: Left: Three-component mixture density with equal variances (solid line) and kernel density estimate based on $h_c(3)$ (dashed line) for the log-data (logarithm to the base 10) for 2003. Right: QQ-Plot of the log-data for 2003 against the quantiles of the normal mixture (three components, equal variances) together with least squares fit (dashed line).

2.2.3 Discriminant Analysis via Posterior Probabilities

Mixture models are routinely used for discriminant analysis, see e.g. Fraley and Raftery (2002). In our analysis of the cross-country income distribution via mixtures, once we have a mixture fitted to the cross-country income distribution, each observation can be assigned posterior probabilities which give the probability of the observation to belong to each of the components in the mixture model.

Consider the log-income distribution in 1976. In Section 2.2.2, we fitted a three-component normal mixture

$$f_Y(y;\hat{p}_1,\hat{p}_2,\hat{\mu}_1,\hat{\mu}_2,\hat{\mu}_3,\hat{\sigma}) = \hat{p}_1\phi(y;\hat{\mu}_1,\hat{\sigma}) + \hat{p}_2\phi(y;\hat{\mu}_2,\hat{\sigma}) + (1-\hat{p}_1-\hat{p}_2)\phi(y;\hat{\mu}_3,\hat{\sigma}), \quad (2.4)$$

where the parameter estimates are given in (2.3). This yields three levels of income which we label poor, middle and rich, with indices $1,2,3$. The posterior probability of an observation y to belong to group j, $j = 1,2$, is equal to

$$p(j;y) = \frac{\hat{p}_j\phi(y;\hat{\mu}_j,\hat{\sigma})}{f_Y(y;\hat{p}_1,\hat{p}_2,\hat{\mu}_1,\hat{\mu}_2,\hat{\mu}_3,\hat{\sigma})},$$

and $p(3;y) = 1 - p(1;y) - p(2;y)$. Therefore, we do not merely assign an income level to each country, but rather a probability distribution, which makes transitions from one group to the other much more transparent.

If one wishes to assign a single number to each country y, one has several possibilities. One is the maximum a-posterior estimate (MPE), which assigns to observation y the j, $j \in \{1,2,3\}$, such that $p(j;y)$ is maximal. One can also determine the thresholds $t_{j,j+1}$, $j = 1,2$, for the values of y at which the MPE changes between the state j and $j+1$, by solving the equations $p(j,t_{j,j+1}) = p(j+1,t_{j,j+1})$, $j = 1,2$, yielding the (in model (2.4)) unique solutions

$$t_{j,j+1} = \frac{\hat{\mu}_j + \hat{\mu}_{j+1}}{2} + \hat{\sigma}^2\frac{\log(\hat{p}_j/\hat{p}_{j+1})}{\hat{\mu}_{j+1} - \hat{\mu}_j}, \qquad j = 1,2.$$

If the weights $\hat{p}_1$ and $\hat{p}_2$ are sufficiently close, the values $t_{j,j+1}$ will indeed be between $\hat{\mu}_j$ and $\hat{\mu}_{j+1}$, in which case they may be properly interpreted. For example, for the year 1976 we get $t_{1,2} = 3.32$ and $t_{2,3} = 3.83$, which on the original scale correspond to the values 2089.30 and 6760.83, respectively. In 1976, by maximum a-posterior estimation there are 46 countries in the poor group, 42 countries in the middle group and 36 countries in the rich group.

Another (more informative) possibility is the posterior mean (PM) of y, which is defined as $p(1;y) + 2p(2;y) + 3p(3;y)$, a number between one and three. In our situation, since the choice of the values $1,2,3$ is arbitrary, this should not be interpreted as a mean but rather as a refined one-number summary of the posterior distribution. For example, if the PM of y is 1.3, then the country will belong to group 1, but will have a tendency toward group 2. A tedious but straightforward computation shows that the posterior mean in model (2.4) with equal $\hat{\sigma}^2$ is a monotonically increasing function of y. Thus, one can uniquely determine thresholds $s_{j,j+1}$, $j = 1,2$, for which the PM is equal to $i + 1/2$. Solving these equations numerically for the parameters in 1976 yields the values 3.32 and 3.84.

2.2.4 More Flexible Mixtures and Model Checking

In Sections 2.2.2 and 2.3.1 we restricted the model class of finite normal mixtures to have equal variances. There are two major technical reasons for this restriction.

First, maximum likelihood inference in mixtures of normal distributions with distinct variances becomes technically difficult since the likelihood function is unbounded. This can be overcome by restricting the range of the estimates, but the true (unknown) parameter must satisfy these restrictions.

Second, if distinct variances are allowed, the posterior analysis is no longer consistent. In fact, higher observations can have smaller MPE or posterior mean than smaller observations, if the variance of components with smaller mean are much larger than those with higher mean. Thus, a posterior analysis does not make sense for such general models.

Nevertheless, in the following we briefly investigate what happens if we drop the assumption of equal variances. Figure B.3 gives density estimates and QQ Plots for the fits with distinct variances for the log-data in 1976. Compared to the kernel estimate, the density of the three-component normal mixture looks somewhat overfitted in the third component. The QQ Plot is similar to that in Figure B.2 for equal variances, with less deviation in the upper tail but more deviation in the lower tail. The AIC and BIC for the three component models with equal and distinct variances are also about equal.

For the log-data at the end of the observational period in 2003, the estimated density of the normal mixture with distinct variances (Figure B.4) looks a little better than that with equal variances (Figure 2.2) when compared to a kernel estimate, though both seem appropriate. The QQ Plots (Figures 2.2 and B.4) are very similar. However, the AIC and BIC are rather in favor of the more complex model.

However, the standard deviation σ of the third component is about twenty times smaller than the σ parameters of the other two components. This makes the model inaccessible to posterior analysis. For example, posterior analysis would assign the USA to the second group. Therefore, in the analysis we stick to the model with equal variances discussed in Section 2.3.1, since it already provides an adequate fit to the data, and allows the analysis of the interdistributional dynamics via posterior analysis. Furthermore, we indicate that both models are not rejected with high p-values when compared to nonparametric fits via the Kolmogorov-Smirnov test. Moreover, note that use of the model with three distinct variances would not change anything about the conclusion that three components are indeed required.

As in Paap and Dijk (1998), one could also use distinct parametric distributions in each component. We chose not to do so since we wanted to emphasize the selection of the number of components. If we allowed distinct parametric models for the components for distinct numbers (i.e. two and three) of components, the models, which would no longer be nested, could not be compared properly. However, this approach could be further pursued in the future.

2.2.5 Parametric and Nonparametric Kernel Density Estimation

When using parametric models such as the finite mixture models above, care must be taken to avoid (strong) misspecification and hence misleading results. Therefore, one often additionally considers nonparametric estimates such as kernel density estimates, and investigates whether the results are similar. Indeed, one can formally compare parametric and nonparametric estimates in so-called goodness-of-fit statistics, which are based on the L_2 or L_∞ distance between the estimators (Fan 1994). Less formally, one can simply visually compare the estimates, as we choose to do here.

However, also nonparametric estimates do not "always" work. Indeed, the cross-country income distribution is concentrated in lower regions, and then has a rather long, small tail at the upper end. For example, in 2003 most values are $< 10^4$, but there is a tail up to $4 \cdot 10^4$ (cf. Figure B.5). Such a shape can lead to a rather poor performance of kernel estimates with a global bandwidth (cf. Wand and Jones 1995, p. 36). As an illustration, we therefore also fitted a transformation kernel density estimate (Wand and Jones, 1995, p. 43) based on the log-transform to the data (cf. Figure B.5). Evidently, the two nonparametric estimates differ strongly, as the usual kernel density estimator puts too much mass to the tails. This leads to the emergence of the second peak in the "twin peaks" phenomenon of the cross-country income distribution, which is thus mainly an artifact of direct kernel density estimation with global bandwidth of heavy-tailed data. Also note that the usual kernel estimator has a boundary problem at 0 (cf. Wand and Jones 1995, p. 46). However, note that the transformation kernel density estimator is quite similar to the three-component log-normal mixture.

Instead of using a transformation kernel density estimator, one can also work directly with the log-data. In order to illustrate that testing the number of components can yield more refined results than nonparametric methods, we apply Silverman's test to the log-data in 2003. Let us first briefly recall Silverman's test. Formally, a *mode* of f_X (and similarly of the kernel estimator $\hat{f}$) is a local maximum of f_X (or $\hat{f}$). Silverman (1981) showed that the number of modes of $\hat{f}$ is a right-continuous, monotonically decreasing function of the bandwidth h if the normal kernel is employed for K: $K(x) = (2\pi)^{-1}\exp(-x^2/2)$. This allowed him to define the k-critical bandwidth $h_c(k)$ as the minimal h for which $f(\cdot;h)$ still just has k modes and not yet $k+1$ modes. Based on the notion of the k-critical bandwidth, Silverman (1981) proposed a bootstrap test for the hypothesis

$$\tilde{H}_k : f \text{ has at most } k \text{ modes} \qquad \text{against} \qquad \tilde{K}_k : f \text{ has more than } k \text{ modes},$$

where in our context, $f = f_X$ (or $f = f_Y$, the density of logarithms $y_i = \log(x_i)$).

The results of Silverman's test for the year 2003 are displayed in table B.2. Here one typically proceeds iteratively by testing $\tilde{H}_k$ for increasing k, starting with $k = 1$, until one finds k such that $\tilde{H}_k$ cannot be rejected with a given level α (e.g. $\alpha = 0.05$). Concerning the log-incomes and their density f_Y, the hypothesis $\tilde{H}_1$ cannot be rejected at a 5% (or even 10%) level. However, the corresponding p-value is still comparatively small. Note that this result does not mean that $\tilde{H}_1$ is true, only that there is not enough evidence to reject it on a level of 5% (or 10%). However, if one continues the analysis, one can clearly reject $\tilde{H}_2$ (p-value < 0.001), but $\tilde{H}_3$ has a high p-value of 0.45. Thus, there is some evidence of three modes in f_Y, but none of only two modes. The associated density estimates with the critical bandwidths are displayed in Figure B.6 (right).

As an illustration we also applied Silverman's (1981) test to the original income data x_i. The hypothesis $\tilde{H}_1$ is clearly rejected with a p-value of < 0.001, and the hypothesis $\tilde{H}_2$ is not rejected with a high p-value. Thus, the procedure stops at $k = 2$, strongly indicating two modes. However, observe Figure B.6 (left). It shows (boundary corrected) plots of the densities with bandwidths $h_c(1)$ and $h_c(2)$. For $h_c(2)$, the third mode (which is not statistically significant according to Silverman's test) is about to occur in the two highest observations of the distribution (at about $35 \cdot 10^3$). Thus, the kernel density estimator is about to put a spurious mode into the tail, and all that Silverman's test tells us is that this mode is indeed spurious.

2.3 Results

2.3.1 Selecting the Number of Components

Applying the methodology above to the time range from 1970 to 2003 for the 124 countries for which we have consistent GDP data yields some surprising and telling insights into the evolution of the cross-country distribution of income. Table 2.1 displays the results of the modified likelihood ratio test for one vs two components and two vs three components as well as the AIC and BIC model selection criteria for the respective fitted models ranging from 1 to 4 component mixtures (all having equal variances). First of all, we note that two components are always preferable to one. In 1970 we cannot reject the hypothesis of two vs three components, however, over the first years of the 1970s the p-values are decreasing and by 1976 the modified likelihood ratio test rejects a two component model at a level of 5%. This is also supported by the values of the model selection criteria AIC and BIC, which initially are in favor of a two component model, but over time switch toward the three component mixture model. In summary, our analysis shows that starting with a two-component (twin-peak) mixture distribution in 1970, in between the "rich" and "poor" components, in the middle of the 1970s a third component evolves in the cross-national distribution of income, thus resulting in a three-component mixture model. All subsequent distributional analysis is based on the three component mixture model from 1976 to 2003.

2.3.2 Evolution of the Cross-Country Distribution of Income

Table B.3 summarizes the main distributional characteristics of the three component mixture model after 1976. The first three columns display the weights p_1, p_2 and p_3 of the three components in the mixture model, which can be directly interpreted as the percentage of data, i.e. the relative number of countries, ascribed to a certain component. As can be seen in Figure B.7, the percentage of data ascribed to the first "poor" component, despite small variation, dropped slightly over time from initially 37.9 percent in 1976 to 35.7 percent in 2003. In comparison, the second component weight gained slightly over time from 33.8 percent to 35.3 percent, leaving the third component weight largely unaltered (28.4 percent in 1970 and 29 percent in 2003). Hence, the relative number of countries ascribed to each component is rather stable over the given observational period.

Regarding the log-income data, it can be observed that the mean of the first component did not grow, but rather experienced stagnation and even slight decline. In comparison, the mean of the

Table 2.1: Component tests and goodness of fit, 1970-2003

	One Component		Two Components			Three Components			Four Components	
Year	AIC	BIC	p of 1 vs 2	AIC	BIC	p of 2 vs 3	AIC	BIC	AIC	BIC
1970	152.47	158.12	0.001	142.64	153.92	0.868	145.88	162.81	145.27	167.84
1974	159.30	164.94	0.001	149.64	160.92	0.243	149.45	166.37	149.46	172.02
1975	157.47	163.11	0.001	147.49	158.77	0.171	146.47	163.39	146.40	168.97
1976	159.72	165.36	0.001	149.72	161.00	0.048	145.80	162.73	145.43	167.99
1980	167.20	172.84	0.000	155.68	166.96	0.037	151.21	168.14	155.21	177.78
1985	173.07	178.71	0.001	162.51	173.79	0.023	156.95	173.87	157.43	179.99
1990	183.20	188.84	0.001	172.40	183.68	0.006	163.84	180.77	164.47	187.03
1995	200.08	205.72	0.001	189.17	200.46	0.004	179.83	196.75	183.83	206.39
2000	204.57	210.21	0.000	192.40	203.68	0.000	173.05	189.97	173.23	195.80
2003	206.50	212.14	0.000	191.62	202.90	0.000	173.58	190.50	174.50	197.06

second and third components clearly increased over the given time period from 3.59 to 3.73 and 4.08 to 4.33 respectively. The standard deviation parameter σ of the three components remains also rather stable over the given time period. However, these model parameters are harder to interpret on the logarithmic scale. Therefore, we also computed the mean and the standard deviation of the log-normally distributed components for the original income data.

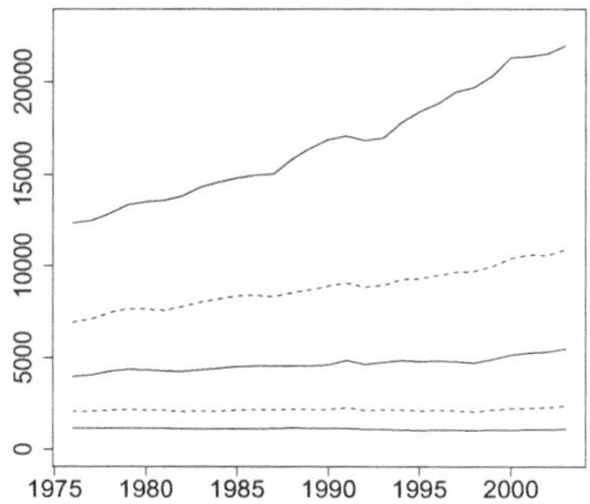

Figure 2.3: Means of the distinct groups (solid lines). Income levels where the maximum a-posterior estimates switch from one group to the other (dashed lines).

Observing Table B.3 and Figure 2.3 we note that the mean GDP per capita of the countries belonging to the first component decreased slightly over time from \$1147 to \$1128. The countries belonging to the second component saw a strongly increasing income from on average \$3998 to \$5504 which corresponds to an overall 37 percent increase between 1976 and 2003. However, over the same period the countries in the third (the richest) component experienced an increase of mean income from \$12335 to \$21938 (increase of 77 percent). Hence, from 1976 onwards the countries in the poorest component experienced stagnation in or even slightly declining average income. Moreover, despite the clear emergence of a third "transitional" component in the middle of the 1970s, the mean income gain experienced in this component is not sufficient to facilitate any catch-up to the third "rich" component, which in turn improves not only its absolute, but also its relative position. Thus, the three components of our model of the cross-national distribution of income per capita actually diverge over time. This leaves slightly over 1/3 of the poor economies in a poverty trap, whereas slightly over 1/3 of the 124 countries, "the middle group", experience growth, but not fast enough to catch-up with the rich countries club, which consists of little less than 1/3 and which improved its absolute and relative position. Thus, one may claim that the cross-national distribution of income is not converging.

and Equatorial New Guinea even improve by one component and are the only three Sub-Saharan African Country that display upward mobility. However, these few encouraging examples are not enough to change the Sub-Saharan stagnant and very poor growth record.
Unsurprisingly, most Western countries belong firmly to the 3rd component displaying hardly any change in their posterior probability mean. It is mainly their growth record which accounts for the increase in the 3rd component mean. Eastern Europe lost in particular after the breakdown of the Iron Curtain, but had resurging growth, which lead to a rather stable position in between the 2nd and the 3rd components over time. Morocco and Egypt show the success of some Arabic countries, whilst Iraq is the extreme opposite and is the country which lost most over the time period 1976 to 2003.
Overall, the country specific data and posterior mean helps to explain the development of the cross-national distribution of income from 1976 to 2003. The following general picture emerges: First, Sub-Saharan Africa accounts mostly for the lowest component which remains stagnant and "poor". Second, the emergence of the "transition" component is mostly due to the growth spurt of the Far East and the relative decline of Latin America. The contrary growth experience accounts mainly for the relatively slow growing mean of the 2nd component. Whilst most Far Eastern countries grow fast enough to catch up with the richer countries of the 3rd component, this is not the case for most of Latin America, which experienced disappointing growth records in particular in the 1980s. Thus, the overall cross-national income distribution does not display absolute cross-national average income convergence, but rather divergence over time, despite the fact that some countries, in particular in the Far East, are rapidly catching-up. However, in the global picture this is counteracted by the relatively poor growth record of Latin America and the average income stagnation in most parts of Sub-Saharan Africa. In particular, almost all of Sub-Saharan Africa seems to be stuck in a poverty trap in which the unit under scrutiny, the national economy, is not capable to deliver any form of sustained per capita growth. However, our data also shows that some of the most populous countries, in particular India and China, are doing extraordinarily well. Thus, the global (and not cross-national) income distribution, which takes into account the distribution of the income within countries as well as the sizes of their populations, might indeed be converging.

2.4 Conclusions

Previous investigations on the twin-peak phenomenon in the world´s cross-country distribution of income were mostly based on nonparametric kernel density estimates, in particular concerning the number of modes of such estimates.
In this essay we use finite mixtures in order to investigate the cross-country income distribution, since *a.* the number of modes depends on the scale (original or logarithmic) whereas the number of components in the mixture does not, *b.* finite mixtures allow for an accurate analysis of the intra-distributional dynamics by using posterior probability estimates, *c.* components in the mixture arguably correspond better to income clubs in the distribution than its modes and *d.* the heavy tail of the cross-country income distribution on the original scale can cause a somewhat limited performance of direct nonparametric kernel density estimates. Furthermore, we

argue that the number of components in the mixture model should be determined by statistical hypothesis testing and model selection.

In contrast to the twin-peaks literature, we find evidence for an emerging intermediate component in the 70s, resulting in a three-component distribution from 1976 onwards. This alone is a strong indication of divergence within the distribution and might be an indicator of convergence within groups.

Diverging estimates of the three group means and very different growth rates between the groups support this conclusion. While the mean of the third (richest) component almost doubled from 1976 to 2003, the mean of the second (intermediate) component only increased by 40 percent (corresponding to a very low annual growth rate), and the first (poor) component even stagnated. One should mention that up- and downward movements of countries affect these growth rates. The growth of the third component is slowed down by countries moving up from the second component. Regarding the second component there are positive and negative effects, in which the negative effects outweigh the positive effects, since only a few countries move from the third to the second component. In the first component there should be positive effects from countries coming from the second group, which however are counterbalanced by the poor overall growth record within this component.

The regional differences are remarkable. While many Asian countries managed to catch up to the third component, the opposite is true in the case of Latin American countries. Sub-Saharan Africa seems to be stuck in the first component and looses more and more contact with the other groups. The very populous countries China and India on the other hand performed extremely well. This fact would foster convergence in a global distribution of income which takes population size and within country inequality into account (i.e. Sala-i-Martin, 2006).

A possible application of our methodology, beyond the conclusions already drawn in this essay, would be a classification of countries according to their mean income, as an alternative concept to the most prevalent "poor, middle and rich" classification of the World Bank. Indeed, the maximum posterior estimates can be used to assign countries to certain groups. Due to its statistical nature, this approach would be less policy dependent than current approaches. The boundary points of income, separating the three groups, from our point of view currently somewhat arbitrarily obtained, could be replaced by the incomes where the maximum a-posterior estimate switches. For the year 2003 these are $2405 and $10859, respectively (PPP, base year 2000). However, our main aim was not to suggest a new system of classification of countries, but rather to obtain a better understanding of the cross-national distribution of income, its development, number of components and its intra-distributional dynamics over the past decades.

Essay 3

Income Distribution Dynamics and Pro-Poor Growth

3.1 Introduction

Over the past decade increased attention has been given to the evolution of global income inequality and the connected questions of global welfare and poverty development. In the light of an ever intensifying globalization of the world economy, a rising concern is to identify global and regional winners and losers of this process. From a welfare point of view, the question might not be whether globalization generated economic growth per se, but rather how pro-poor this growth was or in other words which section of the global income distribution benefited most from the relatively successful global growth record of the past decades.

Recent papers model the global income distribution, or a distribution limited to major economic players, by taking into account the underlying national income distributions (Dowrick and Akmal, 2005; Milanovic, 2002; Chen and Ravallion, 2004; Chotikapanich et al., 1997; Bourguignon and Morrisson, 2002; Quah 2002; Bhalla, 2002; Sala-i-Martin, 2006). In fact, an objective way to construct the global income distribution from the distinct national income distributions is as a population weighted finite mixture of the national income distributions. Intuitively, if one picks at random an individual with a certain income from this global income distribution, one first randomly draws the country it comes from (with probability equal to that countries proportion of the world population), and then obtains its income from the corresponding country income distribution. The main task in this approach is to determine the national income distributions.

A debate continues concerning the data sources on which estimates of the income distributions should be based. Two main concepts have been used so far. The first approach, labeled Concept 2 by Milanovic (2006), combines national accounts income data with household survey inequality data to derive a global income distribution. The second approach (labeled Concept 3 by Milanovic 2006) is purely based on income and inequality data from household surveys.

---

based on joint work with Hajo Holzmann and Julian Weisbrod.

Both approaches have their associated merits and serious caveats, which have been discussed extensively in the literature (Milanovic, 2006; Sala-i-Martin, 2006; Ravallion, 2003; Deaton, 2005).

As far as the poverty headcount is concerned, the headcount for the $2 per day poverty line of studies based on Concept 2 (Sala-i-Martin, 2006) roughly corresponds to the headcount of the $1 poverty line estimated under Concept 3 (Chen and Ravallion, 2004). A simple reason is that the ratio of household level income to national account is about $1/2$ (cf. Deaton, 2005). However, it is beyond the scope of this essay to discuss the advantages or disadvantages of certain poverty lines. We decided to stick to the $1 and $2 US (PPP) poverty lines applied to income as it makes our results comparable to those by Chen and Ravallion (2004) and Sala-i-Martin (2006).[1]

Sala-i-Martin (2006) argues that from the methodological point of view, one should use nonparametric kernel estimates instead of parametric models for the country income distributions, since these do not assume any specific shape for the income distributions. While we agree with it on a methodological basis, in our opinion nonparametric modeling would require actual income data for all countries under consideration, and on a comparable basis. Thus, nonparametric modeling would be the method of choice when using Concept 3 by Milanovic (2006). Using Concept 2, Sala-i-Martin (2006) estimates the national income distributions nonparametrically from the five quintiles. However, we argue that with such data availability, it is not easily justified to be so sophisticated. We therefore prefer to model the national income distributions parametrically as log-normally distributed. The parameters of each country's log-normal income distribution can be determined from its real PPP GDP/per capita and its Gini coefficient (cf. Section 3.2.2). Indeed, when testing for log-normality from the quintiles or even from the deciles, we can reject the hypothesis of log-normality for only less than 0.5% of all countries, and never for one of the population heavy weights China, India, the U.S., Indonesia and Brazil. Therefore, we choose the simpler and arguably more transparent parametric model.

Using this slightly simplified model, we extend Sala-i-Martin's (2006) results to include in particular the important issues of pro-poor growth and of regional inequality. To investigate pro-poor growth, we construct growth incidence curves for several semi-decades, both for the world income distribution as well as for different regional income distributions, specifically the OECD Countries, East Asia and the Pacific, Latin America and the Caribbean, Middle East and North Africa, Eastern Europe and Central Asia, South Asia and Sub-Saharan Africa. For the development of regional inequality, we compute several inequality measures, focusing on Theils' inequality measure which can be decomposed into within and between country inequality.

In the following, we give estimates of the evolution of global poverty and inequality over time, which is a benchmark with respect to other studies (Milanovic 2002; Chen and Ravallion 2004, 2007; Sala-i-Martin, 2006). In addition, we contribute to the ongoing debate in the literature by providing regional and time specific between and within country income inequality based on Theil's measure. Moreover, we discuss semi-decade specific global growth incidence curves, and therefore are able to give a precise description of pro-poor growth. Morevover, we decompose

[1] Furthermore, we show in figure C.2 that any reasonably selected monetary poverty line would show a decline in the poverty headcount ratio as the cumulative distribution function of global income of subsequent time periods dominates over the cumulative distribution function of the prior time period.

the world into the seven main regions mentioned above and investigate the regional variation in poverty and inequality development. Furthermore, we also analyze the underlying regional growth incidence curves, which yield a regionally comprehensive picture of pro-poor growth and of the intra-distributional dynamics in unprecedented detail.

3.2 Methodology and Data

3.2.1 Data

The subsequent analysis is based on two main data sources. Income data are drawn from the Penn World Tables 6.2, which report the real GDP per capita in constant international dollars (chain series, base year 2000), available for most countries. However, for three particularly populous countries, namely Bangladesh, Russia and Ukraine we estimated the initially missing values.[2] Our second data source is the inequality data set by Grün and Klasen (2008) based on the WIDER database.[3] Their adjusted Gini data set derived by estimation techniques has substantive advantages in terms of comparability, as the raw Ginis in the WIDER database are not fully comparable over time and countries.[4] Furthermore, as inequality does not change too dramatically over time, we assume the first real observation of the Gini in any given country to be equal to its initial level of inequality. Starting from this initial level we used a moving average to catch changes in trends of inequality. [5]

3.2.2 Mixtures of Log-Normal Distributions

As stated in the introduction, the national income distributions will be modeled by a log-normal distribution. Formally, the log-normal distribution $LN(\mu,\sigma)$ is defined as the distribution of the random variable $Y = \exp(X)$, where $X \sim N(\mu,\sigma)$ has a normal distribution with mean μ and standard deviation σ. It can be shown that the density of $LN(\mu,\sigma)$ is

$$f(x;\mu,\sigma) = \frac{1}{x\sigma\sqrt{2\pi}} \cdot e^{-(log(x)-\mu_i)^2/2\sigma^2}, \qquad x > 0,$$

and its mean and variance are given respectively by

$$E(Y) = e^{\mu+\sigma^2/2}, \qquad Var(Y) = (e^{\sigma^2}-1)e^{2\mu+\sigma^2}. \tag{3.1}$$

[2]For Bangladesh we calculated the values for the two initial years 1970, 1971 using the average income per capita growth rate of the rest of the decade. For Russia and Ukraine we used the derived (Penn World Tables 5.6) USSR growth rates to estimate the average income for the years before 1990.

[3]We would like to thank Grün and Klasen for providing their data set.

[4]This is mainly due to different methodological approaches and measurement units. The adjustment by Klasen and Grün takes these methodological differences into account.

[5]Unfortunately, there is no reliable inequality data for the populous Democratic Republic of Congo, hence we used the neighboring Central African Republics' Gini as a substitute.

We should briefly discuss the interpretation of the parameters μ and σ, which is different from that of the normal distribution. In fact, from (3.1) one sees that e^{μ} is proportional to the expectation and $(e^{\mu})^2$ is proportional to the variance, and in fact, e^{μ} is the scale parameter of the log-normal distribution, whereas σ is a shape parameter. Since the Gini coefficient is invariant under changes of scale (it does not matter whether income is measured in Euro or in Dollar), it should be independent of μ and only depend on σ. This is indeed the case: The Gini coefficient G of $LN(\mu,\sigma)$ is given by $G = 2\Phi(\sigma/\sqrt{2}) - 1$, where Φ is the distribution function of the standard normal distribution. Therefore, the parameters μ and σ of $LN(\mu,\sigma)$ can be determined from the mean EY and the Gini coefficient G as follows.

$$\sigma = \sqrt{2}\Phi^{-1}\left(\frac{G+1}{2}\right), \qquad \mu = \log(E(Y)) - \sigma^2/2.$$

In summary, the parameters μ and σ of each country's log-normal income distribution are easily determined from the real PPP GDP per capita (EY) and its Gini G.
Let us now formalize how the density of the world income distribution f_W is obtained as a mixture of national (log-normal) distributions. Assuming that there are n countries under investigation and that the (log-normal) density of the distribution of country i is given by $f(x;\mu_i,\sigma_i)$, then

$$f_W(x;\mu_1,\ldots,\mu_n,\sigma_1,\ldots,\sigma_n,p_1,\ldots,p_n) = \sum_{i=1}^{n} p_i f(x;\mu_i,\sigma_i),$$

where p_i is equal to the proportion of country i´s population in the whole population of these n countries.
It has to be stressed that although the density f_W is a simple finite mixture of the component country densities $f(x;\mu_i,\sigma_i)$, this does not transfer to relevant quantities such as the Gini or other inequality or poverty measures: the world Gini G_W is not simply the corresponding finite mixture of the country Ginis G_i. Nevertheless, once the parameters of the density f_W are estimated, it is not difficult to compute the poverty rates as well as percentile specific growth rates numerically from the distribution for any given level of accuracy without sampling. Furthermore, we obtained a number of other inequality and poverty measures by Monte Carlo simulation from f_W. To this end we used a random sample of size 10^6 to obtain the desired accuracy. Since there are no substantial differences between the results of different poverty or inequality measures, we will only discuss the poverty measures by Foster, Greer and Thorbecke as well as the Gini and Theil's measure of inequality. Theil's measure is especially informative since it can be decomposed into separate measures for inequality between and within countries. Our poverty line is set at \$469.9 US (PPP) and \$935.45 US (PPP) a year, which corresponds to the World Bank 1993 poverty line of \$1.08 US and \$2.15 US per day adjusted to our income baseline year 2000 respectively.[6]
Finally, let us remark that, if the world income Y is distributed as f_W, then the log world income $\log Y$ has density

$$lf_W(x;\mu_1,\ldots,\mu_n,\sigma_1,\ldots,\sigma_n,p_1,\ldots,p_n) = \sum_{i=1}^{n} p_i \phi(x;\mu_i,\sigma_i),$$

[6]adjusted to our 2000 base year \$1.08 (1993) per day = \$ 1.287 (2000) per day = \$469.9 per year. In the case of the \$2 line \$2.15 (1993) per day = \$2.562 (2000) per day = \$935.45 per year

where $\phi(x;\mu,\sigma)$ is the density of $N(\mu,\sigma)$. Thus lf_W is simply a finite mixture of normal densities.

3.2.3 Discussion

In this Section we discuss the statistical methodology used for estimating the world income distribution, in particular as compared to the nonparametric approach taken by Sala-i-Martin (2006).
When estimating a country's income distribution from micro data (as in Concept 3 by Milanovic 2006), it is of course well known that even more sophisticated parametric models than the simple log-normal distribution (see e.g. McDonald and Mantrala 1995) can be rejected by appropriate goodness-of-fit tests, and nonparametric modeling is the method of choice.
It is less clear what approach is the best to estimate national income distributions under Concept 2 by Milanovic, when only mean, Gini and quintile data from the distribution are available. In particular, nonparametric kernel density estimation requires the actual income data, and not only some few parameters.
However, Sala-i-Martin (2006) uses Concept 2 and apparently estimates the national income distributions by a kernel density estimator which is not applied to actual income data, but rather to the five quintiles which are treated as "observations". In our opinion, when only certain parameters of the income distributions such as mean, Gini coefficient and quintiles are available, it is natural to employ a parametric model which only uses the parameters available. Of course, the model can and in general will still be misspecified for the actual income distribution, but it is the best we can do with the data at hand.
Since the mean, Gini and the deciles for each income distribution are estimated from huge samples, they will be very close to the true parameters of the underlying distribution. A log-normal model then only uses two of these parameters, namely the mean and the Gini. One can check whether the deciles at least approximately are in accordance with this model by plotting the deciles of the standard normal distribution against the logarithms of the income distribution deciles. These pairs should, at least approximately, lie on a straight line. Note that this is not a QQ Plot in the statistical sense since we plot the (essentially) "true" deciles of the income distribution against those of the standard normal distribution. Figure C.3 shows some plots for the USA, China, India and Brazil for different years. The approximations are reasonably good, although the lowest and in particular the highest deciles typically show some deviation.

3.3 The Global Income Distribution

3.3.1 Inequality and Poverty

Figures C.1 and 3.1 show estimates of the global income distribution as well as of the log-income distribution, determined as discussed in Sections 3.2.1 and 3.2.2, for selected years. Two striking features are apparent: First, the average global income increased drastically over the given time period, and second, the world income distribution has become less dispersed. Interestingly, the 1970s and 1980s still seem to display two distinct modes in the global log-income distribution. However, these "twin peaks" disappear over the years and in particular between 1990 and 2003. Thus, the results clearly show global income expansion and convergence of real global individual income in $US (PPP). The Gini and Theils' inequality measures reported in Table 3.2 confirm this first impression as both measures decline over the given time period, from 0.68 to 0.64 and from 0.88 to 0.80 respectively.[7] The decomposition of Theil's measure shows that this decline in inequality was mainly due to a strong decline in inequality between countries, while inequality within countries even increased. This observation is consistent with a first impression of the biggest countries China and India where inequality increased over time.

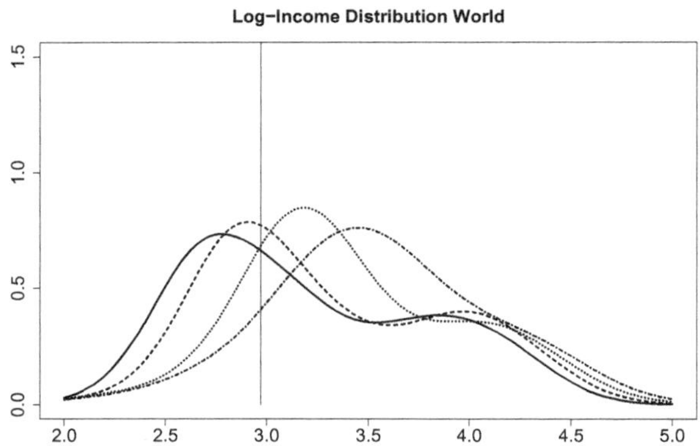

Figure 3.1: Global distribution of log-income. Solid line: 1970, dashed line: 1980, dotted line 1990, dashed-dotted: 2003.

Table C.2 shows the results of the Foster-Greer-Thorbecke (FGT) poverty measures for the poverty headcount and the poverty gap ratio. Furthermore, the absolute number of people below the two poverty lines is reported in Table 3.1. It is apparent that from 1970 to 2003 all measures of poverty, absolute and relative, declined strongly. The percentage of the world population living below $1 a day declined drastically from 21 percent in 1970 to 6 percent in 2003. The reduction of this measure of extreme poverty was particularly rapid in the 1970s and early 1980s as the headcount ratio dropped from 21 percent in 1970 to 8 percent in 1985 which corresponds to a decline of the absolute number of people living with less than $469.9 (PPP, 2000) per year from slightly over 785 million in 1970 to roughly 400 million in 1985. From 1985 to 2003 the headcount fell further to 6 percent which corresponds to about 365 million people living below

[7] We calculated a number of other inequality measures. However, they all show more or less the same overall picture, so we only report Gini and Theil.

$469.9 (PPP, 2000) per year. Moreover, the poverty gap ratio also displays a constant decline over the given time period, hence, not only did the absolute number of people living in extreme poverty fall, but those which remained poor saw their income improved toward the poverty line. The halving of the number of people living in poverty is especially impressive since the world's population almost doubled in the given time period. The results of the $2 poverty line follow a very similar pattern. The headcount declined strongly from 43 percent, almost half the world's population, in 1970 to 14 percent in 2003. The most dramatic decline of the $2 headcount was in the late 1970s and the 1980s from 42 percent in 1975 to 21 percent in 1990. Overall, the absolute number of people who lived below $935.45 (PPP, 2000) per year declined from 1,571 million in 1970 to 893 million, in 2003. Furthermore, the poverty gap or "distance" of those people below the poverty line to the poverty line also declined considerably.

Our findings compare well to other studies measuring global poverty and inequality. Clearly, there are differences in details, but our results are generally reconcilable with the underlying pattern and dynamics observed in other studies. Concerning the poverty headcount rates vis-a-vis Sala-i-Martin (2006) we find higher poverty estimates in the initial years for both $1 and particular the $2 poverty headcount rates. However, over the course of the observational period these differences decline to 0.2 percentage points for the $1 and about 5 percentage points for the $2 poverty headcount rate. Given, as discussed above, that Chen and Ravallion (2007) calculate their poverty rates based on Concept 3, our appropriate benchmark is their $1 compared to our $2 poverty headcount rate. Here, their estimate is higher (about 5 percentage points) over the period from 1981 to 2003. Concerning global inequality, our results for the Gini and Theils' measure of inequality are rather close to those in Sala-i-Martin (2006) and also to all other estimates as summarized in Milanovic (2002).

Thus, our results, as all other studies using various conceivable poverty measures, show a dramatic decline of global poverty in relative and even in absolute terms, although clearly some decades experienced more pro-poor progress than others. In order to get a more refined picture of the underlying dynamics of poverty change we investigate the global growth incidence curves and corresponding rates of pro-poor growth.

3.3.2 Growth Incidence Curves and Pro-Poor Growth

In Figure C.4 global growth incidence curves for different time periods are displayed, which show the percentile specific growth rates over the global income distribution.[8] The main results are also summarized in Table C.3 below. If one considers the entire observational period, it is apparent that the middle percentiles of the global income distribution experienced the highest growth rates. In fact, the growth rate from the 8.5th to the 63.5th percentile of the global population experienced income growth rates above the mean of growth rates of all percentiles, which is equal to 2.3 percent per annum. Thus, the bottom-middle of the global income distribution experienced the fastest income growth, which also explains the declining income inequality and global income convergence. This effect is slightly counteracted by the less than average growth performance of the bottom percentiles (up to the 8.5 percentile), with the poorest percentiles ex-

[8]For a methodological discussion of growth incidence curves see Ravallion and Chen (2003)

Table 3.1: Global and regional population and number of poor people (in thousands).

	Population	Poor ($1)	Poor ($2)	Population	Poor ($1)	Poor ($2)
	World			OECD Countries		
1970	3,693,695	784,540	1,570,698	701,854	33	721
1975	4,070,666	779,835	1,691,192	730,625	8	235
1980	4,437,900	609,085	1,577,463	755,245	2	94
1985	4,832,425	399,595	1,313,699	777,772	2	61
1990	5,255,923	370,810	1,097,183	802,713	1	32
1995	5,660,651	385,708	1,006,770	829,867	3	81
2000	6,052,688	359,184	894,835	854,570	1	27
2003	6,275,048	365,006	893,394	869,918	1	31
	East Asia Pacific			Latin America Caribbean		
1970	1,167,975	530,322	913,422	282,977	20,595	53,936
1975	1,307,614	452,382	946,337	321,049	21,521	54,661
1980	1,419,429	332,907	869,163	360,466	9,450	33,328
1985	1,534,017	125,390	601,954	400,724	12,795	41,643
1990	1,662,816	94,202	414,950	442,008	17,500	53,657
1995	1,776,351	53,042	229,147	482,773	21,805	63,503
2000	1,877,921	38,277	140,236	522,037	23,046	65,913
2003	1,929,034	45,379	158,974	544,279	23,602	67,207
	Middle East North Africa			Eastern Europe Central Asia		
1970	137,202	11,594	32,309	387,557	6,034	16,875
1975	157,584	10,927	32,308	408,977	4,255	13,057
1980	184,880	7,180	26,057	429,959	5,276	15,128
1985	219,384	8,846	29,005	451,243	3,396	12,059
1990	253,947	8,942	29,433	469,334	1,625	7,835
1995	282,784	13,259	31,838	477,391	2,744	15,936
2000	314,504	10,140	30,611	480,881	773	7,564
2003	333,963	16,957	37,634	480,573	670	5,649
	South Asia			Sub-Sahran Africa		
1970	726,192	99,960	353,579	289,938	106,307	176,593
1975	813,860	162,234	421,552	330,957	116,482	195,182
1980	906,662	103,946	377,792	381,259	143,776	232,441
1985	1,009,753	75,083	335,824	439,532	171,901	275,029
1990	1,118,609	46,775	263,634	506,494	200,578	314,139
1995	1,231,644	60,695	285,100	579,841	232,567	370,463
2000	1,346,805	47,109	238,323	655,972	238,775	404,047
2003	1,416,242	36,126	199,439	701,039	242,947	419,153

Table 3.2: Global and regional inequality measures and inequality decomposition

Year	Gini	Theil	Theil Between	Theil Within	Gini	Theil	Theil Between	Theil Within
	World				OECD Countries			
1970	0.682	0.881	0.615	0.266	0.385	0.251	0.020	0.231
1975	0.684	0.887	0.612	0.275	0.377	0.240	0.015	0.225
1980	0.679	0.875	0.608	0.267	0.378	0.244	0.015	0.229
1985	0.669	0.859	0.592	0.267	0.387	0.259	0.019	0.240
1990	0.662	0.848	0.571	0.277	0.387	0.259	0.014	0.244
1995	0.655	0.845	0.531	0.314	0.404	0.284	0.016	0.269
2000	0.646	0.816	0.502	0.314	0.404	0.285	0.019	0.267
2003	0.640	0.796	0.468	0.328	0.407	0.290	0.018	0.272
	East Asia Pacific				Latin America Caribbean			
1970	0.497	0.522	0.269	0.253	0.573	0.620	0.072	0.547
1975	0.509	0.551	0.307	0.244	0.591	0.686	0.048	0.639
1980	0.524	0.583	0.334	0.249	0.540	0.541	0.040	0.501
1985	0.475	0.484	0.257	0.227	0.544	0.558	0.031	0.527
1990	0.495	0.501	0.248	0.253	0.567	0.619	0.034	0.585
1995	0.491	0.482	0.196	0.285	0.582	0.654	0.042	0.612
2000	0.477	0.436	0.150	0.286	0.590	0.677	0.050	0.627
2003	0.504	0.473	0.124	0.350	0.583	0.657	0.048	0.609
	Middle East North Africa				Eastern Europe and Central Asia			
1970	0.551	0.570	0.144	0.426	0.362	0.221	0.048	0.172
1975	0.555	0.572	0.190	0.382	0.357	0.214	0.045	0.169
1980	0.513	0.484	0.089	0.395	0.360	0.220	0.052	0.168
1985	0.505	0.468	0.087	0.382	0.367	0.226	0.062	0.164
1990	0.489	0.439	0.077	0.363	0.368	0.226	0.063	0.163
1995	0.491	0.450	0.116	0.333	0.448	0.356	0.027	0.328
2000	0.506	0.474	0.100	0.374	0.436	0.334	0.034	0.300
2003	0.512	0.480	0.114	0.366	0.441	0.345	0.049	0.296
	South Asia				Sub-Saharan Africa			
1970	0.351	0.207	0.001	0.206	0.637	0.879	0.347	0.532
1975	0.413	0.295	0.002	0.292	0.638	0.859	0.349	0.509
1980	0.375	0.239	0.004	0.235	0.660	0.948	0.411	0.537
1985	0.373	0.238	0.005	0.232	0.666	0.968	0.452	0.516
1990	0.366	0.229	0.006	0.223	0.677	1.027	0.432	0.595
1995	0.396	0.269	0.008	0.261	0.666	1.040	0.442	0.599
2000	0.412	0.295	0.009	0.286	0.663	1.049	0.448	0.601
2003	0.412	0.295	0.009	0.286	0.659	1.033	0.442	0.590

periencing the lowest income growth overall. Furthermore, the global average income grew by 1.8 percent per annum, whereas the median global individual experienced a per annum income increase of 3.0 percent. The rate of pro-poor growth[9] for the $1 per day poverty line exceeds with 2.2 percent per annum the growth rate of the mean by about 0.4 percentage points per annum. Hence, the 34 years from 1970 to 2003 can be termed pro-poor in the relative sense, as the poor experienced higher income growth rates than the average income.[10] For the $2 per day poverty line the period was even more pro-poor as the rate of pro-poor growth with 2.7 percent per annum exceeds the growth rate of the mean with almost 0.9 percentage points per annum and is even greater than the mean percentile growth rate. Hence, the global growth incidence curves over the period from 1970 to 2003 confirm and strengthen our inequality and poverty results above, as they show that over the 34 years the incomes of the poor have grown much faster than the average income. In fact, the bottom-middle income percentiles experienced the highest income growth rates explaining global income convergence, declining inequality and falling poverty headcounts. In order to understand in which era growth was particularly pro-poor, we take a closer look at semi-decade specific growth incidence curves.

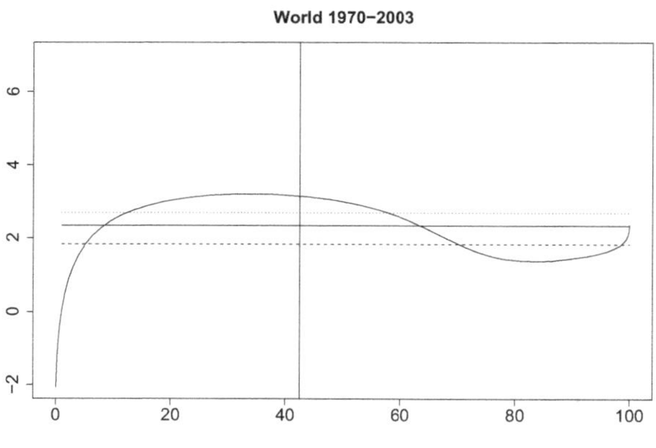

Figure 3.2: Global Growth Incidence Curve 1970-2003. Solid line: Growth Incident Curve, solid vertical line: $2 per day poverty line, solid horizontal line: Mean of Growth Rates, dashed line: Growth Rate of Mean, dotted line: Rate of Pro-poor Growth

For the first half of the 1970s the top and bottom percentiles of the global income distribution experienced the highest growth rate. If one considers the $1 per day poverty line, these years experienced relative pro-poor growth. However, this is not the case, if one applies the $2 per day line, since the bottom-middle of the income distribution experienced only modest growth rates

[9]The rate of pro-poor growth is defined as the average growth rate of the percentiles below the poverty line.

[10]Note: a time span is considered to have been relatively pro-poor if the mean growth rates of the percentiles below the poverty line is larger than the growth rate in mean.

compared to the mean. The second half of the 1970s is characterized by the strongest global growth performance of 2.2 percent per annum in mean income and can be considered relatively pro-poor under the $1 and the $2 per day poverty definition. It is apparent that the bottom half of the distribution had higher growth rates than the average percentile growth rate and thus the bottom-middle of the global income distribution gained the most.

The first half of the 1980s can be considered the most pro-poor over the given time period as the bottom half of the distribution experienced very high growth rates compared to the top percentiles. The mean income grew by only 0.8 percent per annum, but the rate of pro-poor growth was 4.6 and 4.7 per annum for the $1 and $2 per day poverty lines respectively. The second half of the 1980s experienced an increase in the global mean income growth rate to normal 1.9 percent per annum and is characterized by negative pro-poor growth rates for the extreme poor, at -0.9 percent per annum, and growth rates for the poor, at 1.0 percent per annum. This is mainly due to the fact that the very bottom percentiles experienced an income decline, whereas the bottom-middle part of the distribution was doing reasonably well, so the bottom-middle half of the income distribution did catch up further to the upper percentiles. However, it is also important to note that the overall poor percentiles in 1985, which are considered to be poor under the $1 and $2 per day definitions, have been extremely reduced from the previous very pro-poor growth spell. In particular, the bottom-middle percentiles grew consistently, closing the income gap between the developing and developed world, which can also be seen if one looks at the log-income distribution where the two modes start to dissolve over the course of the 1980s.

The 1990s cannot be considered relatively pro-poor. The highest growth rates over the decade are achieved by the inter-quartile percentiles that experience above mean percentile growth rates. This implies further global income convergence over the 1990s, and at the end of the 1990s no hint of a second peak in the global log-income distribution remains. However, these percentiles are no longer considered poor. The overall growth rate of mean income follows the previous decade pattern with the first half being characterized by relatively slower growth rates, 0.7 percent per annum, followed by stronger growth rates of 2.0 percent per annum in the second half. For the first four years in the new millennium the growth rate of mean income has slowed down again to 1.3 percent per annum. The rate of pro-poor growth is below the average income growth rate with the bottom percentiles growing at only 0.5 percent per annum for the $1 per day poverty line and 0.6 percent for the $2 per day poverty line. The highest growth rates are observed in the upper-middle part of the income distribution.

3.4 Regional Income Distributions

3.4.1 Regional Income Distributions

In order to get a more detailed picture, we decompose the world into seven regions which are analyzed separately: the OECD countries, East Asia and the Pacific, Latin America and the Caribbean, Middle East and North Africa, Eastern Europe and Central Asia, South Asia and Sub-Saharan Africa (cf. Table C.1 for the countries belonging to each region).

The income and log-income distributions for these regions, modeled as described in Section 3.2, are shown in Figures C.1 and 3.1. One observes a significant increase in the mean of the income distributions of East Asia and the Pacific and South Asia, whereas Latin America as well as the Middle East and North Africa, which were at the beginning relatively rich regions in comparison to the other developing regions, only saw rather slow progress. In contrast, Eastern Europe and Central Asia is the region which was initially characterized by the lowest inequality levels followed by a sharp increase in inequality after the breakdown of the Iron Curtain. However, due to its relative wealth, the region contributes little to the global poverty count if one considers the $1 and $2 per day poverty lines. Sub-Saharan Africa's distribution hardly shifts at all implying virtually no gains and a relative deterioration compared to the other regions.

3.4.2 Regional Poverty and Inequality Measures

Poverty and inequality measures for these seven regions, which reflect the overall picture above, are reported in Tables 3.1,3.2 and C.2. Indeed, the region with the highest poverty headcount in 1970, namely East Asia and the Pacific, experienced the most breathtaking poverty decline from 78 percent in 1970 to 8 percent in 2003 combined with a strong decline in inequality between countries in this region. Moreover, the absolute number of poor decreased, despite strong population growth, from about half a billion or one billion to about 45 and 160 million for the $1 and $2 poverty definition respectively. Furthermore, Latin America and the Caribbean, as well as the Middle East and North Africa saw their poverty headcounts decline by almost half. However, their absolute number of poor increased slightly under both definitions due to population growth. Moreover, South Asia also experienced a remarkable poverty decline even though less spectacularly and from a lower initial level than East Asia, causing the absolute number of poor to fall from about 100 or 350 million to about 36 and 200 million for the $1 and $2 poverty lines, respectively. This experience was combined with rising inequality from an initially very low level driven by within country inequality. Furthermore, the often lamented case of Sub-Saharan Africa is confirmed by our numbers, as it is the only region which experiences virtually no improvement in any of the measures. This stagnation of Sub-Saharan Africa and relative decline in comparison to all other regions becomes even more apparent if we take a look at the regional decomposition of the absolute number of poor as part of the global population. While the poverty rates remained more or less constant over the years, the absolute number of people living in poverty more than doubled due to population growth from about 100 and 180 million to about 240 and 420 million for the $1 and $2 poverty lines, respectively. Moreover, inequality measures even saw an increase from initially already very high levels, both for within and between country inequality. This implies that Sub-Saharan Africa is nowadays by far the most unequal and poorest region of the world in relative and absolute terms overall. However, as far as within country inequality is concerned Latin America still has to be considered the most unequal region, as seen by the within Theil inequality measure. Furthermore, Eastern Europe and Central Asia contributes little to the global poor if one considers the $1 and $2 per day poverty lines and thus is characterized by very low and slightly declining poverty rates and absolute number of poor combined with strongly increasing within country inequality after the breakdown of the Iron Curtain from initially rather low levels. Finally, for completeness' sake, a quick glance at the OECD countries shows that it basically contributes nothing to the global

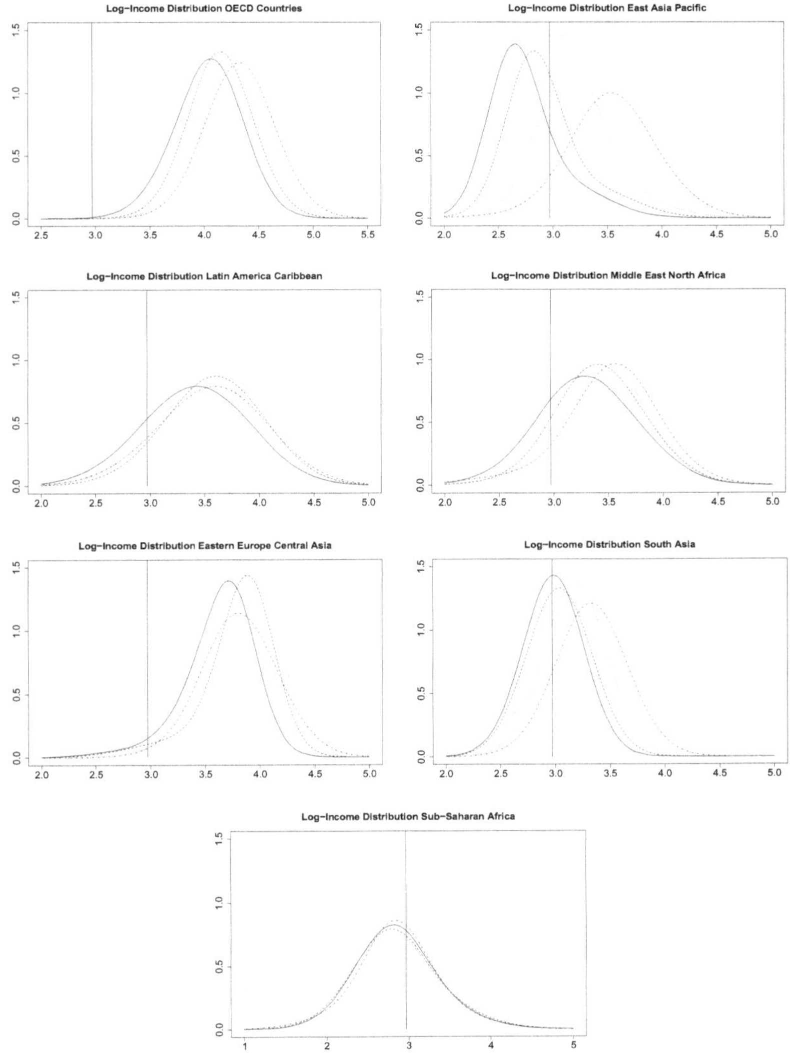

Figure 3.3: Global and regional distribution of log-income. Solid line: 1970, dashed line: 1980, dotted line 1990, dashed-dotted: 2003.

poverty dynamics under the applied definitions.[11] However, the region experienced a marked increase in inequality due to an increase in within country inequality.

3.4.3 Regional Growth Incidence Curves

The poverty and inequality dynamics described above become even more apparent if one takes a closer look at the regional growth incidence curves and results over the entire period as shown in Figure C.5. Moreover, a closer look at the semi-decade specific results conveys an even more detailed picture of the regions' growth experience during shorter time periods.

The OECD Countries. The results for the OECD countries show that even though the average growth rate varied between better semi-decades, such as the late 1990s or late 1970s, and less strong growth periods, as the early 1990s and the early 1980s, the overall intra-distributional growth pattern is very stable. During all semi-decades, except for the start of the new millennium, the growth incidence curves show higher growth rates for the richest percentiles. Thus, the higher the population percentile the higher the income growth rate, with the logic consequence of increasing inequality over time.

Eastern Europe and Central Asia. Eastern Europe and Central Asia is telling a more interesting story as it is much less homogeneous. It is clear from the growth incidence curves that during the first half of the 1990s the bottom half of the regional income distribution saw their income decline drastically, see Figure 3.4. These high negative growth rates, directly after the Soviet Regime's collapse, are causing a slight increase in the poverty rate by 1995. The other semi-decades can be characterized as more pro-poor, except for the very bottom percentiles, accounting for the slightly declining inequality up to 1990 after which inequality increases rather rapidly, before it improves again.

East Asia and the Pacific. The fact that East Asia is by far the most dynamic region and accounts for most of the dramatic global poverty reduction is apparent from a closer look at the regional growth incidence curves. Except for the start of the new millennium, which displays a slow down in the mean of growth rates to about 2.5 percent per annum, and the early 1970s which had around 3 percent, all semi-decades are characterized by a high mean of growth rates of about 4 percent per annum. Furthermore, the early 1980s and 1990s saw most remarkable mean percentile growth rates of more than 6 percent per annum, combined with rates of pro-poor growth of 9.2 and 8.1 percent per annum for the early 1980s respectively (see Figure 3.4); no other region has such a consistently high growth record. From the seventies onwards, the poverty headcount index is steadily declining mainly due to good growth records in the bottom middle of the regional income distribution. In the early 1980s it is in particular the bottom percentiles which grew most rapidly. Moreover, the growth spurt of China, as the region's most populous country, accounts mostly for these very high growth rates, and thus accounts for a major share of the dramatic poverty headcount reduction from 61 percent to 39 percent over a 5 year period. For the bottom half of the distribution the 1990s were rather successful, lowering poverty rates even further from 25 to 8 percent. Moreover, the region is displaying a clear lead concerning the

[11] Clearly neither the $1 nor the $2 poverty line is a very suitable poverty measure for rich countries in general.

overall growth rate in mean, and is therefore the main driving force behind the convergence of the global income distribution.

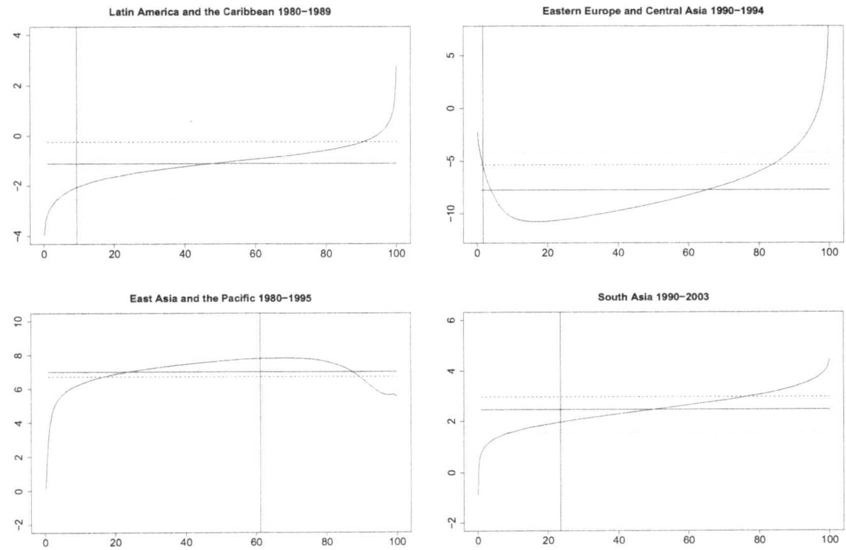

Figure 3.4: Growth Incidence Curves for selected years. Solid line: Growth Incident Curve, solid vertical line: $2 per day poverty line, solid horizontal line: mean of growth rates, dashed line: growth rate of mean, dotted line: rate of pro-poor growth

Latin America and the Caribbean. Latin America saw the second lowest growth rate in mean, which was almost distribution neutral, and is characterized by the third and second lowest rates of pro-poor growth (for the $1 and $2 lines, respectively). Consequently, the poverty headcount dropped only slightly from 19 percent in 1970 to 12 percent in 2003 with inequality remaining high. Hence, Latin America was relatively outperformed in terms of growth and poverty reduction by all other regions except for Sub-Saharan Africa. Despite the overall rather stagnant picture there are some marked semi-decade specific variations. Most pro-poor were the late 1970s, however, the promising high growth rates were not maintained. Thus, the relative deterioration with respect to the other regions is mainly due to the 1980s, which are characterized by negative growth rates except for the very rich percentiles and are thus known as the lost decade in Latin America (compare Figure 3.4). The 1990s again display low positive growth rates in mean, however, the rate of pro-poor growth remains negative in the first half of the decade. Overall, Latin America's growth record is disappointing as poverty reduction could have been much more rapid and a further divergence from the richer regions is apparent.

Middle East and North Africa. Overall, the Middle East and North Africa display a similarly disappointing growth rate as Latin America with equally bad rates of pro-poor growth. In particular, the very low pro-poor growth rate at $1 per day is almost as low as in Sub-Saharan Africa; however, the proportion of the population living below $1 per day is clearly much lower. Over the 34 year time period the region managed to lower its poverty headcount rate from 23 to 11 percent whilst reducing regional inequality slightly. Taking a closer look at the overall growth incidence curve, one can see that the very poor of the region experienced by far the lowest or even negative income growth. However, from about the 10th percentile the growth incidence curves look relatively pro-poor explaining the slight drop in the Gini coefficient and Theil's inequality measure.

Given this overall 34 year development a closer look at the semi-decade specific pro-poor growth rates for the Middle East and North Africa shows a particularly strong fluctuation of the pro-poor growth rates ranging from -13.7 to 8.8 percent per annum and -8.3 to 5.5 percent per annum for the $1 and $2 poverty lines respectively. Whilst the 1970s saw positive and strong growth rates of the poor, the first half of the 1980s, 1990s, and 2000s are characterized by a growth collapse of the poor. In contrast, the second half of these decades saw compensatory pro-poor growth rates, such that overall the region saw a poverty decline and a lower Gini coefficient at the end of the observational period. However, like Latin America the region has been outperformed in terms of growth and poverty reduction by South and East Asia.

South Asia. South Asia is the second most dynamic and populous region of the world over the given time period. Even though growth has not been relatively pro-poor, the overall growth record was sufficiently strong to lower the headcount at $2 per day from half the population to 14 percent, whilst regional inequality saw an increase from initially very low levels due to an increase in within country inequality. In particular, India's growth record accounts for much of the regional dynamics as it is by far the largest country. Even though the early 1970s were characterized by negative growth rates the second half saw very high rates of relative pro-poor growth, initiating a constant poverty decline. The entire 1980s display relative pro-poor growth rates. In particular, during the 1980s the very poorest experienced growth rates of about 3 percent per annum. Average growth rates for the percentiles below the $2 per day poverty line increased from 2.7 to 3.2 percent per annum from the first to the second half of the 1980s respectively. The early 1990s are characterized by a general growth slow down with negative pro-poor growth rates, before growth resurges in the second half of the 1990s and during the first years of the new millennium, however, with only modest gains for the very bottom percentiles (see Figure 3.4). In general, the region's pro-poor and overall growth record is the second major driving force behind global income convergence with India accounting for a large proportion of this income catch-up.

Sub-Saharan Africa. As mentioned above, Sub-Saharan Africa is by far the most troublesome region as it remains virtually stagnant with constantly high rates of poverty and inequality. This is mainly due to the non-existent growth record of the region as a whole and is combined with a worsening of regional inequality at a very high level both within and between countries. This leaves Sub-Saharan Africa in 2003 as the most distinctively poor region in relative and absolute terms, as well as most unequal region in the world. The overall growth rate in mean over the 34 year period is 0.3 percent per annum, with even lower rates of pro-poor growth for both poverty lines with the very bottom of the distribution experiencing even a negative growth record.

Indeed, the semi-decade specific analysis shows relatively successful early 1970s followed by a devastating picture for the late 1970s, 1980s and early 1990s, all of which are characterized by a negative average growth rate and negative or only slightly positive growth rates in mean. Results for pro-poor growth are similar, even though the early 1990s saw the first positive pro-poor growth rates after 15 years. The late 1990s and the start of the new millennium indicate a more encouraging picture. Despite remaining low growth rates at least some slow progress has been made in particular for the poor, which still account for almost 60 percent of the regions' population and experienced positive and for the region unparalleled rates of pro-poor growth. However, over the entire period the region has been virtually stagnant. Whilst it was "only" the second poorest region in the world in 1970, it is by far the poorest region in the world in the new millennium and experienced high relative income deterioration. In fact, about two thirds of the world's extreme poor and about half of the world's poor live in Sub-Saharan Africa nowadays (compare Table 3.1). Hence, it is clear that any serious attempt to further reduce global poverty will fail, if it fails to reach Sub-Saharan Africa.

3.5 Conclusions

In contrast to studies analyzing the polarization of the cross-national average income per capita distribution, this study of the global income distribution as a whole shows strong global income convergence amongst all the world's citizens. We use a simple parametric mixture approach, with log-normal national income distributions and weights determined by the country's population, which appears to be adequate for the data available in the WIDER database. Our results show that the past 34 years witnessed a strong global income convergence accompanied by a drastic decline of global inequality and poverty no matter what conceivable monetary poverty line is applied. Noticeably, overall inequality declined because of declining inequality between countries, whilst inequality within countries increased. Furthermore, the analysis of growth incidence curves shows that the bottom-middle part of the income distribution experienced above average percentile growth rates, which explains the occurring global income convergence. In particular, the late 1970s and early 1980s are characterized by high global rates of pro-poor growth, initiating the rapid decline of global poverty rates.
A regional decomposition of our data reveals that in particular the extraordinary growth record of East Asia and South Asia, which includes the two population heavy weights China and India, accounts mostly for the global income convergence and rapidly declining poverty rates. Latin America and the Middle East and North Africa showed slower but steady progress in poverty reduction. However, their more modest growth experience implies a relative income deterioration vis-á-vis the richer regions and also East and South Asia, and thus, can be seen as a remaining diverging factor in the global income distribution. Lastly, Sub-Saharan Africa has remained virtually stagnant and has become the poorest region in relative and absolute terms, implying a steady divergence and disconnection from the global growth process. Nevertheless, from a global perspective, the observational period is characterized by an unparalleled improvement of income per capita and an unprecedented poverty reduction. This in itself can be considered a great success and is in particular due to the fact that the bottom-middle global income percentiles

managed to catch up to higher levels of income, thus reducing the dispersion of income from a global perspective. On the other hand, the remaining very lowest percentiles also experienced the lowest percentile growth rates, such that the remaining extreme poor might be particularly hard to reach.

Given the high share of global extreme poor and high poverty headcounts in Sub-Saharan Africa it is clear from our analysis that any further massive extreme poverty reduction can be only achieved by pro-poor, or at least distributional neutral, growth in Sub-Saharan Africa. The remaining poor seem to be, if Chen and Ravallion's (2007) rural-urban poverty decomposition is any indication, mostly to be found in rural areas. Thus, any attempt to reduce global poverty even further must focus mainly on fostering growth in Sub-Saharan Africa and on remaining, in particular rural, national pockets of poverty.

Essay 4

EU-ACP Economic Partnership Agreements

4.1 Introduction

Until 2007 the European Union (EU) granted non-reciprocial trade preferences to African, Caribbean and Pacific (ACP) countries. This policy did not comply with the WTO principle of most-favoured treatment and was only temporarily covered by a WTO waiver which expired in December 2007. Under Cotonou the principle of reciprocity was introduced implying that developing countries had to honour trade concessions given by developed trading partners. Hence, in order to avoid distortions of EU-ACP trade new trade agreements, so called Economic Partnership Agreements (EPAs), were negotiated with a target date of January 2008.
The EPAs between the EU and ACP countries are a new approach to promote trade and to achieve more general development goals at the same time. At the core of the EPAs are regional trade agreements between the EU and each of the six regional ACPs. The EPAs intend to support ACP regional integration to create larger regional markets and foster their integration into world markets. While the previous trade preferences for ACP countries were determined unilaterally by the EU, the EPAs are jointly designed in negotiations between the EU and the ACP countries. ACP countries are requested to open to some extent their markets to EU products in return for their access to EU markets. The long-term goal is quasi duty-free and quota-free market access on both sides and simplified rules of origin in the EU. However, the ACP countries have to open their markets to a smaller extent than the EU does (on average 80 percent within 15 years).
Moreover, EPAs give incentives to ACP countries to increase regional trade and cooperation - to replace the previous arrangements that favoured a hub-and-spoke structure discouraging interaction with neighbours. Understandably, some countries are unwilling to cooperate on issues where they might lose. The EU as a third party can provide incentives to strengthen a regional resolve

---

based on joint work with Inmaculada Martínez-Zarzso, Felicitas Nowak-Lehmann D. and Nils Klann.

to enforce cooperation, and help to overcome such differences. Experience shows however, that (north-south) trade liberalization alone does not always promote economic development. EPAs could take a broader approach and try to improve coherence between trade and development. Besides trade of goods the EPAs also include trade in services as well as trade related issues such as investment, public procurement and competition law. While the agreements on trade of goods and services are about mutual, however asymmetric, trade liberalization, the trade related issues follow another objective. They aim to support regional integration by common regional regulation, harmonization and implementation, helping to improve political and economic stability and creating a better business and investment climate. The EU may thus have to subordinate its commercial interests to the development needs of the ACP countries.
In this essay we estimate the potential welfare effects of a trade agreement between the EU and ACP countries for nine African countries: Botswana, Cameroon, Côte d'Ivoire, Ghana, Kenya, Mozambique, Namibia, Tanzania, and Uganda. The contributions to the existent literature on this field are twofold: First, instead of rather arbitrarily choosing elasticities of import demand, we estimate bilateral elasticities between the EU and Sub-Saharan Africa and between the nine African countries and the EU from highly disaggregated data. Second, instead of simulating general scenarios like full, medium or low liberalization, we apply the actual tariff reduction rates recently negotiated between the EU and the African countries to estimate the agreement's welfare effects of trade liberalization for the African countries.

4.2 State of the EPA Negotiations

The EU started EPAs' negotiations with six ACP regions, which were self-defined by the ACP countries in 2003. These regions include the Caribbean (CARIFORUM), Central Africa (CEMAC), South-East Africa (ESA), West Africa (ECOWAS), Southern Africa (SADC), and the Pacific. The trade structure of these regions often reflects dependency on just a few products. Table 4.1 lists the top four exported products of the six ACP regions. In most cases, these products account for at least two-thirds of total exports.

Table 4.1: Top four exports of the six ACP regions

	Top export (%)	Second export (%)	Third export (%)	Fourth export (%)
Southern Africa	Diamonds (42)	Mineral oil (17)	Aluminum (13)	Fish (8)
West Africa	Mineral oil (45)	Cocoa (21)	Fish (5)	Timber (4)
Central Africa	Mineral oil (47)	Timber (23)	Bananas (5)	Cocoa (4)
East Africa	Textiles (15)	Fish (11)	Diamonds (9)	Sugar (8)
Caribbean	Ships (23) a	Corundum (10)	Ethanol (10)	Sugar (8)
Pacific region	Palm oil (36)	Sugar (16)	Copper (13)	Coffee (7)

Ships and aircraft are not actually manufactured in the Caribbean, the statistics also include cases in which ownership of a ship or aircraft has been transferred. Source: EU Commission and BMZ (2007).

The schedule for negotiations was tight, since the WTO waiver expired in December 2007. In most cases this was insufficient time to finalize full EPAs, thus interim agreements were concluded, in many cases on a sub-regional or bilateral level. Negotiations toward full EPAs continue.

The course of negotiations differs between the regions. For the Caribbean region, a full EPA including trade in services has been finalized in December 2007. The agreement implies a market opening of 61 percent within 10 years and 82.7 percent within 15 years. The members are: Antigua and Barbuda, Bahamas, Barbados, Belize, Dominica, Dominican Republic, Grenada, Guyana, Haiti, Jamaica, St Kitts and Nevis, St Lucia, St Vincent and the Grenadines, Surinam, and Trinidad and Tobago.

For Eastern and Southern Africa two sub-regional interim agreements were concluded with the East African Community (EAC) and Eastern and Southern Africa (ESA). The agreement for EAC implies a market opening of 64 percent within 2 years, 80 percent within 15 years and 82 percent within 25 years. The members are: Burundi, Kenya, Rwanda, Tanzania, and Uganda. The extent of market opening differs among the members of the other agreement between 80 percent (Comoros) and 97 percent (Seychelles). The members are: Comoros, Madagascar, Mauritius, Seychelles, Zimbabwe. The other countries of this region can use market access to the EU under the Everything but Arms initiative for LDCs[1]: Djibouti, Eritrea, Ethiopia, Malawi, Somalia, Sudan, and Zambia.

The sub-regional interim agreement for Southern Africa implies a market opening of 86 percent within 2 years except for Mozambique (80.5 percent within one year). The members are: Botswana, Lesotho, Mozambique, Namibia, and Swaziland. Unfortunately South Africa did not enter the agreement yet. From a development perspective it would be extremely helpful if the major economic driver of the region formed part of the agreement. Angola can continue to use market access through Everything but Arms.

In the Pacific region a sub-regional interim agreement has been concluded with Papua New Guinea and Fiji. It implies a market opening of 88 percent within 15 years in the case of Papua New Guinea and 80 percent in the case of Fiji. The other non-LDCs of this region include Cook Islands, Marshall Islands, Micronesia, Nauru, Niue, Palau, and Tonga. Trade in goods is relatively unimportant for this region, the agreement is therefore expected to have its focus on trade in services. East Timor, Kiribati, Samoa, Solomon Islands, Tuvalu, and Vanuatu can use market access under Everything but Arms.

In Central Africa, only a bilateral agreement with Cameroon could be finalized in early 2008. The agreement includes market opening of 80% within 15 years. The remaining non-LDCs of this region are Congo-Brazzaville and Gabon, both continuing to negotiate own stepping stone agreements. Chad, Central African Republic, DR Congo, Equatorial Guinea, and São Tome are granted market access under Everything but Arms.

[1]For Least Developed Countries (LDCs) the Everything but Arms (EBA) initiative has been in force since 2001. The EBA regulation is granting duty-free access to imports of all products from least developed countries to the EU without any quantitative restrictions, except to arms and munitions. Only imports of fresh bananas, rice and sugar were not fully liberalized immediately but are liberalized step by step. This special arrangement for LDCs is not subject to the periodic renewal of the EU's generalized system of preferences (GSP). The GSP applies to all developing countries, but its conditions are less favourable for ACP non-LCDs than those offered under the Cotonou Agreement.

In West Africa, bilateral agreements have been signed only with Côte d'Ivoire and Ghana. The agreements imply market opening of 70 percent within 10 years for Côte d'Ivoire and 80 percent within 15 years for both Côte d'Ivoire and Ghana. The vast majority of exports of the region come from Nigeria which is a non-LDC where exports are dominated by oil and gas. The other countries of this region include Benin, Burkina Faso, Cape Verde, Gambia, Guinea, Guinea Bissau, Liberia, Mali, Mauritania, Niger, Senegal, Sierra Leone, and Togo, all of which are LDCs and can use market access under Everything but Arms.

4.3 Economic Analysis of EPAs

4.3.1 Review of the Literature

Before we proceed to the analytical framework let us briefly summarize the existing literature on EPAs and their potential impact in the ACP countries or sub-regions. The empirical approaches taken in the literature to estimate the potential effects of EPAs differ quite substantially. Some studies are based on computable general equilibrium (CGE) models, whereas others are based on partial equilibrium (PE) models. On the one hand, the CGE studies are more complex and can take the linkages of the economy into account, on the other hand the PE studies allow for more detailed statements on what is to be expected on the sectoral level. CGE models are mostly unfeasible for African countries due to lack of sufficiently detailed data (Milner et al. 2006).

Although there is a considerably body of literature on the EPAs, most papers focus on policy options rather than assess the trade and welfare effects of the EPAs. To our knowledge, five main studies in the recent past have evaluated the impact of the EPAs in a PE framework. In the first study, Hinkle and Schiff (2004) investigate the effects of an EPA on Sub-Saharan African (SSA) countries. They observe that the liberalization of trade in services which can be part of an EPA agreement will benfit SSA in terms of consumer gains in sectors such as transportation, telecommunication and finance.

Karingi et al. (2005), evaluates the gains and losses associated with EPAs for ACP countries. They predict a decrease in the production of natural resources, energy and cotton and production increases in fishing, animal products, livestock, crops, sugar oilseeds, vegetables and cereals for SSA if a Free Trade Agreement (FTA) with the EU was signed. However, in case of full reciprocity production losses in fishing, livestock and vegetables are to be expected. With respect to manufacturing in the SSA countries, Karingi et al. (2005) find a decline in heavy industry, medium tech and low tech industry, clothing and textiles under full reciprocity, but increases in clothing, textiles and agriculture production under a FTA.

Milner et al. (2006) analyze the EPA's impact on Tanzania, Uganda and Kenya. The authors find the expected consumer gains and production losses but, more importantly, they identify Kenya as a country where losses outweigh benefits, mainly due to the fact that Kenya's manufacturing sector will be negatively affected by EU competition.

Busse and Großmann (2007) analyze the impact of EPAs on West African countries. They find that in most cases trade creation effects (more trade with the EU and some African countries)

outweigh the trade diversion effects (less trade with African countries that are not part of the agreement). They also find a negative impact on the government deficit.
Finally, Fontagné et al. (2008) investigate the impact of EPAs for all six ACP regions. Their results show increased exports of vegetal production, livestock, agrifood and textiles to the EU and big increases in imports from the EU (in the range of 20 to 40 percent) in textiles, metallurgy, primary products and other industries. Huge decreases in tariff revenue (70 to 80 percent) are found for all six regions except for the Pacific where the tariff revenue seems to be unimportant.

4.3.2 Theoretical Framework

The theoretical framework is based on Milner et al. (2006). The authors illustrate the welfare effects of preferential trade agreements for a small country member of an initial PTA graphically. These effects arise from the transition of initial preferential trade agreements (PTA) between African countries to Economic Partnership Agreements. Figure 4.1 shows this initial situation of a PTA between an African country (H) and its regional partner (P). With a PTA in force home country demand for imports (D_H) for a good is met by partner supply of exports (S_P), since domestic production capabilities are assumed to be negligible. Two additional flat lines are shown indicating the infinitely elastic supply of the same good from the European Union and the rest of the world (ROW), respectively. Prices P_{EU} and P_{ROW} are given exogenously since the African countries are small in size relative to the EU and the rest of the world and thus are unable to trigger variations in world market prices through shifts in demand.
In the initial phase with the PTA in force country H imposes an ad-valorem tariff on imports from regions not covered by the PTA i.e. global goods. The resulting price increase is taken into account by adding a second global export supply curve S^t_{ROW}. As can easily be derived from the graph imports amount to $0M_2$. These inflows originate both from country P ($0M_1$) and the rest of the world (M_1M_2).
In the given situation country H could benefit from two sources of welfare gains: assuming that P^t_{ROW} is the price level consumers face, this price level undercuts the spending propensity of all consumers left of point B. This fact generates consumer surplus and is also the first source of welfare the country may derive from the initial situation. The import of M_1M_2 of goods from the rest of the world allows for further welfare gains since duties are levied on these goods resulting in state revenue $(a+b)$.
The implementation of an EPA framework removes these tariffs on goods from the European Union whereas duties remain in place for goods from the rest of the world. The implication of such a shift in policy is a reduction of prices for imports from the EU. Consumers would now face a lower price regime indicated by P_{EU} in Figure 4.1.
Several welfare effects are triggered by this pro-European shift in trade policies: Firstly, the drop of the import price from P^t_{ROW} to P_{EU} will displace country H's former trading partner P as a supplier. Goods of the amount $0M_1$ are now imported from the EU. Hence, the EPA framework results in trade creation, represented by area c in Figure 4.1. The lower price P_{EU} also increases imports and thus consumption of the good in question by M_2M_3 (consumer surplus increase by area e (Figure 4.1). This result is the consumption effect of the EPA-driven shift in the trading structure of the country. With tariffs favouring EU imports over goods from the rest of the world

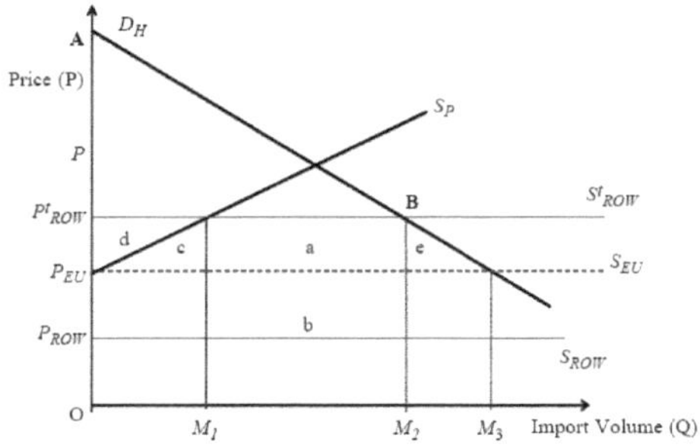

Figure 4.1: Welfare effects of a reduction in tariffs

the bear share of imports i.e. M_1M_2 is now purchased from EU suppliers in place of tapping supply from the rest of the world. The welfare effects of this shift, in terms of trade creation and trade diversion, towards the EPA framework are complex: The EU is a less efficient choice for importing the good in question than the rest of the world. This is indicated by the higher price of EU goods in comparison with suppliers from the rest of the world. The adverse effect of this trade preference is captured by the trade diversion effect amounting to M_1M_2. The consequence of employing a less efficient source for imports generates costs of the amount of area b in Figure 4.1. In addition, since the tariff revenue is not collected anymore, the total tariff revenue lost by the home country is represented by area $(a+b)$ in Figure 4.1. The global welfare effect is ambiguous, and depends on the elasticities of the home demand for imports and the export supply of exports and is represented by the area $(c+d+e)-b$ in Figure 4.1.

These three trade effects, consumption effect, trade creation and trade diversion, associated with a move from a PTA to an EPA usually take place simultaneously. However, for specific sectors (products) it could be that only one or two of the effects occur. As a matter of fact, it is assumed that in sectors for which the EU is the dominant supplier only consumption effects will follow, while in sectors for which the dominant supplier is the rest of the world, also trade diversion occurs. Trade creation together with consumption effects will follow in sectors where another ACP country (in the regional PTA) is a relatively important supplier (providing more than approx. 25 percent of imports).

It can be assumed for sectors in which the EU is the dominant supplier that supply from the rest of the world is more expensive than the supply from the EU and that there are no competitive regional supply capabilities. Thus the consumption effect alone is given by

$$\Delta M^C = \left(\frac{t}{1+t}\right) \varepsilon_M^D M_0^{EU} UV_0^{EU} \qquad (4.1)$$

where t is the current tariff, ε_M^D the price elasticity of import demand, M_0^{EU} the current import volume originating from the EU and UV_0^{EU} the current unit values[2] (prices) from the EU. The associated revenue (ΔR^C) and welfare (ΔW^C) effects are

$$\Delta R^C = -tM_0^{EU}UV_0^{EU} \quad (4.2)$$

$$\Delta W^C = 0.5t\Delta M^C \quad (4.3)$$

The consumption effects with trade diversion are given by the following formulas, where ROW stands for rest of the world:

$$\Delta M^{TD} = M_0^{ROW}UV_0^{ROW} \quad (4.4)$$

$$\Delta R^{TD} = -tM_0^{ROW}UV_0^{ROW} \quad (4.5)$$

$$\Delta M_{TD}^C = 0.5\left(\frac{t}{1+t}\right)\varepsilon_M^D M_0^{ROW}UV_0^{EU} \quad (4.6)$$

$$\Delta W_{TD}^C = 0.25t\Delta M_{TD}^C - 0.5tM_0^{ROW}UV_0^{ROW} \quad (4.7)$$

Finally the consumption effects with trade creation are given by:

$$\Delta M^{TC} = M_0^{PTA}UV_0^{PTA} \quad (4.8)$$

$$\Delta M_{TC}^C = 0.5\left(\frac{t}{1+t}\right)\varepsilon_M^D M_0^{PTA}UV_0^{EU} \quad (4.9)$$

$$\Delta W_{TC}^C = 0.5t\Delta M_{TC}^C + tM_0^{PTA}UV_0^{PTA} \quad (4.10)$$

We will focus on the welfare and the revenue effects of trade creation, trade diversion and consumption. With this aim, sectors will be classified into three different categories according to who is the dominant supplier in this sector.

According to the outlined analytical framework and in line with the empirical studies discussed in Section 3.1, the effects that will follow after an EPA between the EU and ACP countries or subgroups are now summarised. First, a lowering of tariffs in the ACP region (among African countries) will lead to trade creation in this region as long as ACP prices are below EU prices. EU countries will also profit from better access to ACP country markets because import tariffs will have to be lowered for EU manufactured and agricultural exports as part of an EPA agreement. Given that the EU is strong in producing manufactured exports a rise in EU exports of manufactures to ACP countries is expected.

Second, lower tariffs of manufactured products will put producers of manufactures (the import substitution industry) in ACP countries under pressure. ACP countries with bias towards producing products such as machinery, chemicals, pharmaceuticals, plastic, glass, and ceramics will lose given that a lowering of import tariffs will make them less competitive and will reveal weaknesses in productivity or innovation. Third, better EU access to the ACP market can lead to a displacement (trade diversion) of previously competitive African neighbours if they are not part of the agreement and if their price is above the EU price in the aftermath of the EPA agreement.

[2] Unit values are defined as import value divided by import volume.

Fourth, the consumers in all the ACP countries (in the very poor, poor and richer ACP countries) will profit from cheaper imports (trade concessions for the EU countries) and from a greater variety of incoming imports. Finally, with respect to government revenue, state earnings from levying duties will decrease in all ACP countries and new sources of revenue creation or taxation will have to be found.

4.4 Empirical Analysis and Policy Implications

4.4.1 Elasticities for Import Demand

Import demand elasticities are an important ingredient of ex-ante analyses of trade reforms. Price elasticities are crucial for assessing the effects on trade volumes of changes in relative prices following tariff cuts arranged in the negotiations of regional trade agreements. Price elasticities are also necessary to estimate ad-valorem equivalents of quotas or other non-tariff barriers. In addition, trade policy is frequently determined at high levels of disaggregation, whereas existing import demand elasticities are only available, for many countries, at a high aggregation level. This divergence can lead to serious aggregation biases when calculating the impact of trade policies. We aim to fill in this gap by estimating import demand elasticities for the nine African countries considered in this essay. We are thus able to build up on the methodology employed in Busse and Großmann (2007) where elasticities are pre-defined in place of being estimated from the data.

In the recent past, trade economists often used trade elasticities from the surveys of the empirical literature put together by Stern et al. (1976) and by Sawyer and Sprinkle (1999). More recent attempts to provide disaggregated estimates of import demand elasticities include Shiells et al. (1986), Shiells and Reinert (1993), Blonigen and Wilson (1999), Marquez (1990, 1999, 2002), Broda et al. (2008) and Gallaway et al. (2003), Kee et al. (2004) and Hertel et al. (2007). Import demand elasticities for many African countries at disaggregate level are not available in the existent literature.

In order to evaluate the impact of the EPA agreements and its associated welfare effects across different African countries, one would need to have a consistent set of trade elasticities, estimated using the same data and methodology. If possible, it would also be desirable to use a framework for the estimation that is consistent with trade theory. Hence we will specify and estimate a demand for imports that relates changes in the quantity of imports to changes in relative prices. This follows the Armington assumption (based on the differentiation of products with respect to their origin and the imperfect substitution in demand between imports and domestic supply).

The share of import in domestic demand is related to their relative prices. An increase in domestic price level creates an incentive for increasing the share of imports. The specification of the import demand is,

$$\frac{M}{D} = \left(\frac{P_D}{P_M}\frac{\delta}{1-\delta}\right)^{\sigma} \tag{4.11}$$

Table 4.2: Import demand elasticities by country

	EU 25	Sub-Saharan Africa	Non-Manufacturing SSA (HS 0 - HS 2)	Manufacturing SSA (HS 3 - HS 8)
Uganda	-0.967***	-0.707***	-0.522**	-0.684***
	(0.036)	(0.051)	(0.171)	(0.053)
Tanzania	-0.815***	-0.845***	-0.935***	-0.809***
	(0.047)	(0.046)	(0.110)	(0.053)
Mozambique	-0.911***	-1.044***	-1.189***	-1.005***
	(0.034)	(0.040)	(0.148)	(0.043)
Ghana	-0.870***	-0.589***	-0.638***	-0.566***
	(0.055)	(0.050)	(0.122)	(0.055)
Côte d'Ivoire	-1.588***	-0.774***	-1.059***	-0.722***
	(0.088)	(0.076)	(0.200)	(0.081)
Botswana	-0.997***	-0.479***	0.222	-0.487***
	(0.057)	(0.123)	(0.639)	(0.126)
Kenya	-1.063***	-1.054***	-1.122***	-0.989***
	(0.042)	(0.037)	(0.106)	(0.041)
Namibia	-0.796***	-0.941***	-1.009**	-0.932***
	(0.047)	(0.126)	(0.331)	(0.138)
Cameroon	-1.484***	-0.677***	-1.084*	-0.631***
	(0.079)	(0.091)	(0.503)	(0.085)
Fixed Effects		YES		
R-squared	0.74	0.7	0.563	0.746
AIC	68891.6	64701.41	15520.4	46040.21
BIC	69031.07	64840.83	15633.85	46173.75
N	17123	17079	4034	12315

Note: *** denotes significance at 1 percent level, ** denotes significance at 5 percent level. Standard errors are reported in brackets.

where M denotes import quantity, D denotes domestic demand (quantity produced and sold in Home), P_D is the domestic price and P_M is the world market price, and σ is the price elasticity of imports, that will be estimated.

A way of extending this formulation to the multiple countries (regions) case consists of using bilateral trade at highly disaggregated level. Given this scenario two different types of elasticities can be considered: The elasticity for the choice between imports from different exporters and the elasticity of the choice between imports and domestic production. Since domestic production is not available at a high level of disaggregation we choose to use the first elasticity. We will follow a difference in difference approach that is described below. The import demand equation for multiple exporters and products is,

$$\frac{M_{ijk}}{M_{ilk}} = \left(\frac{\delta_{ijk} P_{ijk}}{\delta_{ilk} P_{ilk}} \right)^{\sigma_{ik}} \tag{4.12}$$

where i denotes the importing country and j, l the exporter countries (regions), k denotes a specific product (HS six digits level). M are import quantities and P are import prices. We use import unit values as a proxy for import prices. By taking logarithms of equation 2 and adding and error term and importer fixed effects we derive the empirical model as,

$$\log\left(\frac{M_{ijk}}{M_{ilk}}\right) = \sigma_{ik}\log\left(\frac{\delta_{ijk}P_{ijk}}{\delta_{ilk}P_{ilk}}\right) + \alpha_i + \varepsilon_{ik} \tag{4.13}$$

where α_i are importer fixed effects and $\varepsilon_i k$ is the error term which is assumed to be well behaved. Equation (13) is estimated with trade data for 2005 (Import values and import quantities are from COMTRADE) for nine importers (Uganda, Tanzania, Mozambique, Ghana, Côte D'Ivoire, Cameroon, Botswana, Kenya and Namibia) and three exporting regions (European Union, Sub-Saharan Africa and World). Two versions of equation (13) are estimated. The first one considers imports from the EU with respect to imports from the world as the dependent variable, whereas the second considers imports from SSA with respect to imports from the world.

Table 4.2 presents the aggregate price elasticities of import demand for each importer country. Tables D.1 and D.2 summarize the trade elasticities for imports from the EU25 and other Sub-Saharan African countries at HS one digit levels. In essence, the disaggregated data used to generate the measures reported in Tables D.1 and D.2 avoids imposing identical parameters on all classes of goods. It is interesting to note that many of the elasticity estimates across import categories within specific countries have very similar magnitudes.

In the subsequent analysis we use the estimated elasticities at the highest level of disaggregation possible. However, for some countries and sectors there were no sufficient data to estimate a significant elasticity (for example Namibia and HS 0). In these cases we use elasticities obtained at a more aggregate level.

4.4.2 Welfare Effects of an EPA

Combining the trade elasticities of Section 4.1 and the analytical framework of Section 3.2 we are now able to assess the potential welfare effects of full trade liberalization and of the interim agreements. For this purpose we use trade data from UNSD COMTRADE and tariff data from UNCTAD TRAINS at a very high level of disaggregation (HS six digits level). As a first step we assume that tariffs are completely abolished with the PTA. The overall welfare effects for the nine African countries are shown in Table 4.3.

It should be noted that a tariff reduction to zero describes a rather extreme case which would stand at the very end of an EPA process. Nevertheless, we find that in most cases trade creation effects outweigh trade diversion effects. Only Côte d'Ivoire, Ghana and Kenya experience relatively small welfare losses compared to their overall trade volume. Botswana, Cameroon, Mozambique and Namibia are identified as biggest winners under a full trade liberalization scenario.

The overall welfare effects can be decomposed into partial effects for manufacturing (HS codes 3 to 9) and non-manufacturing (HS codes 0 to 2) products. Generally speaking one could say that manufacturing products account for most welfare losses, while the welfare effects are positive for the non-manufacturing products (except for Ghana).

Next we calculate the short-run (five years) and long-run (end of the transition period) welfare effects of a trade liberalization given the actual interim agreement's tariff reduction rates. The

Table 4.3: Potential welfare effects of a full liberalization

	Botswana	Côte d'Ivoire	Cameroon	Ghana	Kenya	Mozambique	Namibia	Tanzania	Uganda
All products									
Consumption	60.68	7256.11	8697.38	5741.34	2100.62	201.68	14.87	2051.05	255.62
Diversion	-275.91	-27390.91	-20974.4	-148269.2	-76760.92	-10679.51	-957.47	-34380.72	-29559.79
Creation	163104.9	15341.28	160097.8	44628.63	46416.89	77565.48	247078.9	57062.36	63250.91
Total	162889.7	-4793.51	147820.8	-97899.23	-28243.41	67087.65	246136.3	24732.69	33946.74
in %	5.35%	-0.08%	5.42%	-1.12%	-0.55%	4.27%	10.07%	1.01%	2.06%
Revenue	-1905.1	-155502.2	-120378.9	-431936.9	-228347.2	-30452.95	-2530	-124062.5	-90611.12
Non-manufacturing									
	Botswana	Côte d'Ivoire	Cameroon	Ghana	Kenya	Mozambique	Namibia	Tanzania	Uganda
Consumption	0.05	4776.27	3706.5	2409.5	392.53	174.19	0.39	803.24	64.01
Diversion	0	-3573.07	-2475.2	-48474.36	-18658.82	-6729.47	-7.59	4166.82	-9814.55
Creation	2732.19	14751.16	157731.9	21264.45	33953.27	23711.4	48884.25	30997.74	38892.14
Total	2732.24	15954.35	158963.2	-24800.4	15686.97	17156.12	48877.05	35967.8	29141.6
in %	0.25%	0.50%	11.41%	-0.93%	0.97%	3.47%	8.06%	5.93%	5.36%
Revenue	-1.02	-49668.85	-27310.43	-156580.8	-63662.65	-16543.93	-255.84	-25342.99	-24412.88
Manufacturing									
	Botswana	Côte d'Ivoire	Cameroon	Ghana	Kenya	Mozambique	Namibia	Tanzania	Uganda
Consumption	60.63	5185.24	4990.88	3331.95	1957.71	27.49	14.48	1259.08	193.23
Diversion	-277.18	-28087.53	-18499.2	-100101.2	-74954.16	-3950.04	-949.89	-49647.93	-26536.35
Creation	155662	1838.58	2365.87	23892.61	15487.33	56173.02	198141.8	33311.55	29379.43
Total	155445.4	-21063.71	-11142.45	-72876.6	-57509.12	52250.47	197206.4	-15077.31	3036.31
in %	7.90%	-0.64%	-0.84%	-1.20%	-1.40%	4.72%	10.73%	-0.65%	0.21%
Revenue	-1904.07	-135051.4	-93068.45	-275978.5	-202989.4	-13909.02	-2274.16	-121830.8	-80569.24

Note: Units are 1000 USD.

Table 4.4: Long-run welfare effects of a tariff reduction according to the interim agreements

	Botswana	Côte d'Ivoire	Cameroon	Ghana	Kenya	Mozambique	Namibia	Tanzania	Uganda
All products									
Consumption	60.68	5934.84	8697.38	3558.57	1347.27	18.23	14.87	74.09	116.85
Diversion	-275.91	-22364.72	-20974.4	-70937.72	-40832.61	-1519.43	-957.47	-28107.73	-15822.8
Creation	163104.9	14498.93	160097.8	9754.32	10849.89	36287.77	246991.2	17725.59	11739.78
Total	162889.7	-1930.95	147820.8	-57624.84	-28635.44	34786.57	246048.6	-10308.06	-3966.17
in %	5.35%	-0.03%	5.42%	-0.66%	-0.50%	2.17%	10.07%	-0.35%	-0.20%
Revenue	-1905.1	-120689.2	-120378.9	-202055.1	-117753.8	-5681.96	-2354.41	-61453.07	-38126.76
Non-manufacturing									
	Botswana	Côte d'Ivoire	Cameroon	Ghana	Kenya	Mozambique	Namibia	Tanzania	Uganda
Consumption	60.67	2620.05	3735.52	1691.15	349.96	9.53	0.66	34.8	4.5
Diversion	-11.96	-3721.01	-3464.15	-21493.68	-1481.43	-272.33	-7.59	-905.99	-818.37
Creation	8194.93	13312.04	157913.9	3371.19	1249.85	6109.72	56474.26	2126.61	1533.12
Total	8243.64	12211.08	158185.3	-16431.34	118.38	5846.91	56467.32	1255.43	719.25
in %	0.69%	0.37%	11.02%	-0.58%	0.01%	1.05%	7.89%	0.18%	0.12%
Revenue	-1329.63	-33049.63	-29870.22	-71332.81	-6907.59	-1222.45	-86.97	-2483.71	-2071.51
Manufacturing									
	Botswana	Côte d'Ivoire	Cameroon	Ghana	Kenya	Mozambique	Namibia	Tanzania	Uganda
Consumption	0	3510.4	4961.86	1691.15	997.31	8.71	14.22	39.29	112.36
Diversion	-265.21	-18877.95	-17510.25	-21493.68	-39351.18	-1247.1	-949.89	-27201.75	-15004.42
Creation	150199.3	1564.66	2183.87	3371.19	9600.04	30178.05	190464	15598.98	10206.65
Total	149934	-13802.89	-10364.53	-16431.34	-28753.83	28939.66	189528.4	-11563.48	-4685.42
in %	8.12%	-0.44%	-0.80%	-0.58%	-0.73%	2.77%	10.97%	-0.51%	-0.34%
Revenue	-575.47	-90044.52	-90508.66	-71332.81	-110846.2	-4459.51	-2267.44	-58969.35	-36055.25
	10 years	17 years	18 years	17 years	28 years	13 years	10 years	28 years	28 years

Note: Units are 1000 USD.

results are shown in Tables D.3 and 4.4, respectively. Table 4.4 shows that in the long-run only Botswana, Cameroon and Namibia realize their full potential of welfare gains under the interim agreements. The welfare effects for Mozambique are still positive though smaller than in the full liberalization scenario.
The welfare losses of Côte d'Ivoire, Ghana and Kenya under the actual tariff reduction rates are smaller compared to a full liberalization. The effects are now close to zero for these countries, implying that the trade effects of the agreements can be considered more or less neutral. Also for Tanzania and Uganda the predicted welfare effects are close to zero, although the full liberalization scenario suggests that both countries have potential for welfare gains through trade liberalization.

4.5 Conclusions

Overall, we can conclude that a tariff reduction for imports from the EU has no or a slightly positive effect for the African countries in our study. One should note, that this welfare effect can not be interpreted as the total effect of an Economic Partnership Agreement. On the contrary, these effects can be seen as a price to maintain preferential access to EU markets which is compatible to WTO rules. Even a small negative welfare effect due to tariff reduction would not imply that EPAs have a negative impact on African countries. Falling back to GSP would certainly be more disadvantageous for those countries than an EPA. However, other aspects besides tariffs are also important for the potential development success of the EPAs. The interim agreements have to be extended with development components comparable to the Caribbean agreement.
With respect to the loss in tariff revenues, shown in the fourth row of Table 5, although the losses are always compensated by consumption and trade creation effects except for the countries that experience welfare losses (Côte d'Ivoire, Ghana, Kenya, Tanzania and Uganda), this is a very important issue in practice. Tariff revenues contribute, on average, by 2 percent to the GDP - in some cases even up to 6 percent-for Sub-Saharan African countries. Given that trade with the EU accounts for 40 percent of total trade, lower tariffs would imply a stiff decline in government revenues, as our estimates also confirm. Two steps could be taken to resolve this problem. First, ACP countries should be allowed to open their markets to a smaller extent than the EU and with appropriate transition periods, as already acknowledged by the present state of the EPAs or interim agreements. Second the lost tariff revenues should be replaced by increased tax revenues through reforms of domestic tax systems and tax administration.
Certainly, the EU profits the most from making the pre-2008 EU-ACP trade relations WTO compatible. We therefore argue that these additional profits on the EU side should be used for development cooperation. A more radical approach in terms of the tariff losses in Africa would therefore be for the EU to provide budget support to the most affected countries during a predetermined transition period. Such transfers could help African countries to cope with the financial burden of transition costs and offset revenue losses caused by tariff reductions. For companies to reap the full potential of export markets African countries are also well-advised to dedicate some attention to creating a supportive environment for potential exporters. This may include efforts to improve relevant factors such as infrastructure or the legal framework. EU countries could

enhance the development impact of EPA policies by contributing to these improvements through financial or technical assistance. This assistance may also entail helping to establish a sound tax system which replaces tariff collection as a pivotal source of income for the government of African countries. In accordance African countries should make an effort to ensure that their tax collection scheme is able to compensate the losses incurring from tariff reduction. This also entails the improvement of tax administration to ensure reliable tax collection. Hinkle and Schiff (2004) suggest improving the countries ability to collect indirect taxes such as value added taxes in order to compensate losses incurring from tariff reductions.

Comparing the revenue losses under the full liberalization scenario and the long-run interim agreement scenario reveals that revenues were a dominant issue when selecting the products for exclusion. In the case of Tanzania and Uganda the protection of tariff revenues was certainly paid with welfare losses. Overall it is interesting to note that infant industries and welfare arguments did not receive enough attention compared to tariff revenues.

In order to improve the welfare effects, both for countries which are already profiting from a complete tariff offset as well as countries which would loose from a complete tariff offset, products and sectors which suffer from negative welfare effects could be identified and excluded from trade liberalization. Moreover, the exclusion of products from liberalization could be motivated by infant industry arguments or by their importance for government revenues. Only a limited proportion of products can be excluded from liberalization. Therefore we argue that the protection of infant industries should be chosen over the protection of government revenues. The tariff reduction tables of the interim agreements should be evaluated from this perspective.

Essay 5

Political Institutions and Human Development

5.1 Introduction

Since Sen (1983, 1988, 1991, 1999, 2000, 2003 etc.), we are aware of the fact that development is a very encompassing and broad concept. Development as a whole depends on each individual's capabilities. Capabilities define the freedom to choose a valuable life in accordance with individual preferences. This approach inspired the emergence of a pluralist and integrative conception of "human development" and its operationalization in the form of UNDP's Human Development Index. Among other dimensions, income, but also health and education, enable people to shape their lives in line with their desires. The aim of this paper is to discuss the contribution political institutions can make to enhance human development.

Political institutions are an appealing topic of research as they organize social, economic and political life. Hence, an obvious question would be what kinds of institutions do this job best. From an ideological perspective, democracy seems to be the right political system because at the end of the day, its beneficiaries are politically free as well as they are free to take decisions about their lives. Therefore, democracy is also considered an end of the political development process and a piece of the puzzle of the more comprehensive picture of human development (Sen 1999a,b, 2000). But whether democracy indeed has a positive impact on economic and human development is not a trivial question - neither from a theoretical nor from an empirical perspective. With regard to theory, three major debates are circling around the instrumental value of democracy for economic development:

First, there seems to be a controversy concerning the contradictory effects of property rights protection and redistribution in a democracy on growth and well-being. There might be a trade-off between growth-enhancing property rights protection and equalizing, market-correcting redistribution. On the one hand, property rights protection is a necessary condition for an increase

---

based on joint work with Maria Ziegler.

in the overall wealth of a nation (Acemoglu et al., 2001, 2002). But whether all members of this nation can benefit from it highly depends on redistribution as well. On the other hand, the probably adverse effects of redistribution on the savings rate, growth and the labor market and the related effects on the overall living standard of the population including non-income human development come to mind. Moreover, in democracy, corporatism may lead to lock-in effects and a decreasing reform capacity. This danger, together with the fact that elites in democracies tend to produce inefficient policies supports positions like the Lee-Hypothesis[1]. These positions state that autocratic regimes are the more efficient systems to tackle market failures, to stimulate economic growth and as a consequence to improve human development (Alesina and Rodrik, 1994; Barro, 1996; Acemoglu and Robinson, 2008).

A second debate revolves around causation: Is democracy cause or consequence of the development process? A third field, which is linked to this second point, is a range of discussions that focus on factors that impede or foster democratic systems to work well. It is not obvious what the conditions are under which democracies will display a positive effect - given they are supposed to have one. Examples of these enhancing or impeding factors are the level of economic development itself, inequality, country-specific and historical factors, education and social fragmentation (Lipset, 1959; Barro, 1999; Alesina et al., 1999; Bourguignon and Verdier, 2000; Acemoglu et al., 2002; Alesina and Ferrara, 2005; Acemoglu et al., 2008; Acemoglu and Robinson, 2008; Miguel and Gugerty, 2005; Keefer and Khemani, 2005; Collier, 2001).

Empirical research studies give no clear answer to the above questions. Persson and Tabellini (2006) and Rodrik and Wacziarg (2005) show that in case of economic growth the efficiency argument in favor of autocratic regimes does not withstand empirical investigations. Others, on the contrary, find a moderately negative or nonlinear relationship between democracy and growth (Barro, 1996; Tavares and Wacziarg, 2001; Minier, 1998). When studies focus on redistribution, i.e. the effect of political systems on income inequality or on the provision of public goods and the size of the public sector, results are less ambiguous (Boix, 2001; Gradstein and Milanovic, 2004; Persson, 2002; Stasavage, 2005; Persson et al., 2000). In general, they support the view that redistribution might be higher under a democratic regime. But if this is the case, the question still remains whether this redistribution is beneficial to economic and non-income related human development.

Concerning the non-income dimensions of human development, there is again uncertainty about the effects of democracy. There are only very few studies empirically investigating the links between political systems and measures for the non-income dimensions of human development. Whereas some find a positive relationship between democracy and human development (Besley and Kudamatsu, 2006; Franco et al., 2004; Tsai, 2006), others find less evidence for this influence (Ross, 2006). These research efforts are either confined to the sub sample of developing countries (Tsai, 2006), to only one of the non-income dimensions of human development (Besley and Kudamatsu, 2006; Franco et al., 2004; Ross, 2006) or to a cross-sectional focus leaving out developments over time (Tsai, 2006; Franco et al., 2004). Moreover, these investigations, while having in mind potential conditions influencing democracy's performance, only include these

[1]The hypothesis that authoritarian rule is beneficial to economic growth was named after the former president of Singapore, Lee Kuan Yew (Sen 1999b).

requisites as simple controls in their regression models and not interacted with some institutional measure.
In this paper, we want to extend the latter strand of research in the following ways: First, we theoretically discuss why democracy is supposed to have a positive impact on human development. Linked to this field of interest is the question whether democracies, besides their intrinsic importance for the development process, fulfill a constructive and instrumental role giving people the opportunity to express, to form and aggregate their preferences and thus to steer public action in an efficient and effective manner (Sen 1999a). Particularly, we base our argumentation on the redistributive aspect including public goods provision, not the property rights aspect of democracy. We argue that with respect to the quantitative as well as to the qualitative dimension of redistribution and public goods provision, any democracy will perform better than an otherwise equal autocracy; thereby, we rely on implications of the median voter theory and arguments provided by Sen. Although redistribution is often seen as a disturbing factor leading to inefficiencies, we want to clarify why it is redistribution in democracies that makes a difference in non-income human development outcomes compared to autocratic regimes. We also empirically try to find evidence of whether living in a democratic or an autocratic political system makes a difference in the level of education and health, which we take as proxies for non-income human development.
Second, we theoretically identify and empirically investigate the prerequisites for the functioning of democracy as such with respect to the provision of public goods and services that foster human development.[2] This allows us to account for heterogeneity in human development across democratic regimes.
Third, we include the time dimension of the data and all countries on that data is available into our empirical analysis to fully exploit all the information which is available.
Our results indicate that democracy is favorable for human development even after controlling for the level of economic development. But contrary to the theoretical reasoning there is no clear evidence for the factors that according to the literature are supposed to influence democracy's performance. It seems to be democracy itself - rather independent from the circumstances - which has a positive effect on human development. It is in particular remarkable that democracy's performance seems not to depend on a certain level of economic development.

5.2 The Political Economy of Democracy and Human Development

The following remarks serve to clarify the relationship between political institutions and human development. Recurrence on institutionalist theories provides a link from political institutions to the living standard of the population. This link is given, foremost, by the redistributive policies an institutional system produces. The median voter theory predicts that democratic systems are characterized by a higher level of redistribution than autocracies. Consequently, the median

[2]Consequently, we do not try to explain democratization but the dependence of democracy's performance upon other factors once it is in place.

voter theory gives insights into the quantitative dimension of redistribution. Arguments provided by Amartya Sen capture the qualitative part of redistribution and permit to extend the median voter theory by stating that democratic institutions make redistribution more responsive to the needs of the society, i.e. that redistribution translates into a public spending for transfers, goods and services that increase the wealth of the society. To complete our theoretical discussion, we address the issue that the fulfillment of the predictions made by the median voter theory and Sen depends on several requisites that influence any democracy's performance.

5.2.1 How Can Political Institutions Influence Human Development?

Institutions attract a lot of attention in the mostly interdisciplinary studies of differences in the wealth of nations. Questions range from institutional effects on the one-dimensional perspective of economic development to the multidimensional view on human development. However, there still seems to be a bias in favor of the economic side of the coin (Knack and Keefer, 1995; Hall and Jones, 1999; Acemoglu et al., 2001, 2002; La Porta et al. 2004).[3] This reflects the preference, which is probably justified, for the economy as the major driving force of the development process and the resulting focus on the property rights angle of institutions. We want to complete this picture and focus on the redistributive side of institutions and the non-monetary components of human development.

With regard to institutions, the existing literature leaves the impression that there is not enough precision concerning the term "institution" itself. There is a big use of performance indicators measuring the extent to which certain institutional systems function, e.g. when it comes to political stability or governance issues (Gradstein and Milanovic, 2004).[4] Such performance indicators then are often mixed up with public policies. However, both the performance and the policies are the output of underlying structures and procedures as well as contextual factors. These underlying (formal) structures and procedures can be subsumed under the heading political system. This is what we understand by political institutions.

According to the rational choice strand of the new institutionalism in political science or the field of new institutional economics and political economy, political institutions make the rules which govern the political game (e.g. Peters, 1999; Persson and Tabellini, 2000). They do not only determine via electoral rules the actors and preferences which can access the political arena and get heard. They also provide the means to aggregate those preferences by establishing procedures for decision-making and distributing political power, i.e. the right to decide (Persson, 2002). The common output of institutions and preferences are policies. Although actors and other environmental constellations may change over time, policies in general will reflect the political institutions that produced them (Persson and Tabellini, 2006; Peters, 1999). We distinguish between two types of policies that may be favorable to human development: policies for the protection of property rights and policies for redistribution.

[3] A famous controversy in this context is the Geography vs. Institutions debate in the explanation and prediction of economic development (Acemoglu et al. 2002; Grimm and Klasen, 2008).

[4] See for example the Worldwide Governance Indicators (Kaufmann et al., 2007).

Policies for the protection of property rights encourage economic investment and contribute to economic development and economic growth (e.g. Acemoglu et al., 2002). Growth is assumed, under certain conditions, to increase the welfare of the population by reducing poverty (Klasen, 2004). Policies for redistribution have an equalizing impact on the distribution of wealth in a society. Especially through broad-based programs and the provision of public goods and services, market failures shall be compensated and normative, social optima be achieved. The matching of society's and an individual's needs with an adequate redistribution scheme and an appropriate public provision of goods and services provides a more direct link between political institutions and human development than property rights protection. Of course, one might argue as we already mentioned in the introduction that there might be a trade-off between growth-enhancing property rights protection and equalizing, market-correcting redistribution. Nevertheless, the focus of this paper will be on policies with a redistributing character which aim at better health and education for the population as a whole and especially for those groups - the poor - who would otherwise have only limited access to these goods as these are not sufficiently provided by markets.

If we assume that via these channels policies will affect the level of human development, if we especially focus on redistributive policies and moreover, if policies mirror the political system in which society is steered according to certain political decisions, then the following question emerges: Which political systems are more appropriate to produce market-correcting redistributive policies that will additionally match the needs of society and therefore will advance human development?

The answer is democracy. Democracy is conceived as a political system whose structures and procedures permit the rule of the people. Of importance are free and repeated elections, political competition, rule of law, political and civil liberties. These component parts frame public debate and deliberation that deal with the management of society. Carrying forward our reasoning, democratic political systems are assumed to be the most appropriate systems to ensure a redistribution that fulfills societal demands.[5] Although redistribution from the rich to the poor and vice versa exists in both autocratic and democratic systems, the following theoretical arguments make us believe that redistribution from the rich to the poor is more pronounced and set at a higher level in democracies.[6] One of the most famous theoretical arguments is the model of Meltzer and Richard (1981). The median voter hypothesis states that in democratic governments the median voter is the decisive voter. The more his income falls short of the average income of all voters, the higher the tax rate, i.e. redistribution he will decide. Therefore, government spending should be larger and social services more extensive in democratic regimes - if the majority of the voting public lives at the bottom of the income distribution and only a small part enjoy richness (Keefer and Khemani, 2005). In contrast, in authoritarian systems, the distribution of wealth does not play a decisive role. All or a substantial part of the electorate is excluded from the decision-making process, and this is precisely the point to avoid the redistributive consequences of democracy. As a result, the average size of the public sector remains quite small (Boix, 2001)

[5]Democracies are considered to perform best on both dimensions: property rights protection and redistribution. Whether the one or the other is more important depends on people's preferences and the formal and informal face of the considered democracy.

[6]See for example Gradstein and Milanovic (2004) for an empirical study finding evidence for this linkage.

although there are examples of autocracies with a commitment to a relatively large public sector and universal well-being.

The fact that there is more redistribution in democratic regimes does not mean that redistribution is aligned with societal demands. In other words, voting alone does not solve the aggregation problem resulting from different individual preferences. Thus, a second question related to the qualitative dimension of redistribution emerges: Why are democratic governments more responsive to the needs of the citizenry compared to autocratic ones? According to Sen (1999a,b), democracy - behind its "intrinsic" value - is of eminent importance for the process of development because of the "constructive" and "instrumental" role it plays in the formation and aggregation of values, needs and preferences and their translation into well-designed policies benefiting the society. Political and civil liberties - for example those related to free speech, public debate and criticism, as constituent parts of a democratic regime - permit the formation of preferences and values as well as access to the relevant information. Consequently, a better understanding of societal needs is possible. Democratic procedures then facilitate the transmission of these needs into the political arena where decision power is distributed amongst legitimate representatives of the society as a whole.[7]

However, in the "pursuit of political objectivity" and through the facilitation of "public reasoning", democracy not only helps to construct policies that are matched to the needs of its citizens (Sen 2004). It is also instrumental and protective because control mechanisms such as free and repeated, competitive elections and the compliance with the rule of law principle reduce discretionary and corrupt behavior of those representatives who hold political power. Democracy provides the incentives to create responsibility and accountability that induce political-administrative leaders to listen and to act on behalf of the society they represent (Sen 1999a,b).

In an autocratic regime a usually small, ruling elite dictates the will of the people from above. This is frequently accompanied by a repression of the political opposition and the prohibition of free expression and opinion impeding the conceptualization of the volonté générale. The state apparatus is (mis-)used in favor of the welfare of the ruling elite. Political measures with a redistributing character increasing the welfare of the bottom quantiles of society are implemented not because of institutional structures but either due to ideological reasons and/or to a level that will help autocrats remain in power and to increase their own wealth (Olson, 1993; McGuire and Olson, 1996). Responsiveness, representation, accountability and the selection of competent political and administrative staff thus are uncommon in autocratic regimes (Besley and Kudamatsu, 2006). Summarizing, whereas democracies quantitatively and qualitatively perform better than autocracies in terms of redistribution, there is no clear relation between inequality and societal needs on the one hand and redistribution on the other hand in autocracies, except for those, generally socialist ones, with a special commitment to universal welfare. In general, this leads to a lower level of human development in autocratic systems.

[7]The latter means that otherwise disadvantaged groups, whether they are minorities or a broad mass of poor people in a developing country, get a voice and the opportunity to be heard and represented. In cases of direct democracy or democracy at a local level, these groups even decide for themselves.

5.2.2 What Determines Public Service Provision Especially in Democracies?

The formal existence of democracy does not guarantee that it functions in the idealized manner described above. Democratic regimes might display a lot of heterogeneity concerning the benefits for human development. This is the case when certain factors impede or enable that the relationships predicted by the median voter theory or Sen's theory can be observed. These factors then hamper or foster the performance of democracy with regards to the satisfaction of societal needs. Problems could arise if for certain reasons - located either at the agenda setting, the policy formulation, the implementation or evaluation phase - the allocation of public expenditures is inefficient.[8] What are the reasons for an ineffective allocation of public resources, especially in democracies? Or more general, what are those factors that will influence the operation of a democratic regime either in a positive or in a negative direction?

Our approach to explain heterogeneity in any democracy's performance follows the suggestion by Keefer and Khemani (2005) and hence differs from other studies that focus more on the pre-conditions for democracy or democratization (e.g. Lipset, 1959; Glaeser et al., 2007).[9] Following our theoretical reasoning, the necessary timing of the presence of the respective factors is treated here as simultaneous. Their interaction with democracy at one point in time influences the output, the policies in form of public goods' provision, and the outcome, the level of human development.

First, as redistribution and the provision of public goods depend upon the fact whether there is anything to redistribute and to invest in public goods, the performance of a democratic system will be the better the higher the level of economic development is. So the positive effect of democracies on public goods provision will be intensified by the level of economic development.

Second, if citizens are ill-informed, this may lead to insufficient participation, which would be necessary for public reasoning and the expression of 'qualified' needs'. As a result, the quality of responsive government manifesting itself in policies that reflect society's demands and needs decreases. Moreover, accountability suffers from information constraints because voters cannot control politicians' behavior. Education[10] is one of the important factors[11] as it has a potential to alleviate any information problem. Education in this context is not taken

---

[8]Because poor people are highly dependent on public action as they cannot invest their own (nonexistent) private resources, they suffer the most from ineffective government in terms of redistribution and service provision (Keefer and Khemani, 2005).

[9]We do not consider the question whether a country has to be prepared for democracy or whether it is a democracy which lifts the country up to a certain level of development.

[10]We leave out cultural factors here as they are hard to measure. Inglehart and Welzel (2005) emphasize the people's values as equally important as socioeconomic resources and civil and political rights. According to these authors, culture provides the link between economic development and democratic freedom. Without certain values like "human autonomy" or "self-expression values", fostering a priority on self-made choices, human development might not be possible (Inglehart and Welzel, 2005). Moreover, such values are dependent upon a certain level of socioeconomic development. We assume, although this is to be questioned, that the more education people have the more enlightened they are and the more freedom they demand to live the life they value.

[11]Other factors might be a well developed media sector and accountable and institutionalized parties that overtake political education tasks (see Keefer and Khemani, 2005). But it can be easily argued that without a certain level of broad-based education, a media sector will not develop because of a lack of demand (for the role of the media see

as an intrinsic component of human development that we want to explain, but as a means to human development. It is not only in itself a precondition for a higher living standard because it positively affects earnings, health and so on. It is also found to be a requirement for democracies to develop and to persist. Moreover, one can suppose that education leading to conscientious participation raises the quality of democracy. The latter may come to the fore in a more efficient and effective provision of public goods (Lipset, 1959; Glaeser et al., 2007; Keefer and Khemani, 2005).

Social fragmentation can be another factor disturbing the functioning of a democratic system measured by the public goods it provides. Research has found that social fragmentation or, to be more concise, ethnic diversity leads to collective action problems, increased patronage as well as clientelism and in the end to an under-provision of public goods (Alesina et al., 1999; Alesina and Ferrara, 2005; Miguel and Gugerty, 2005). Within democratic systems, social fragmentation may pose problems because mechanisms which would hold the government accountable and responsible are undermined. In socially heterogeneous settings, governments are rewarded on the basis of identity and not on governmental performance (Keefer and Khemani, 2005). Moreover, social fragmentation leads to political fragmentation that from a certain threshold value can result in increasing co-operation problems (Collier, 2001).

The last factor that is in line with our quantity-redistribution argument is income inequality, characterized by a distribution of income where the median income is much smaller than the average income.[12] Hence, the majority of people live at the lower bound of the distribution whereas only a few benefit from being rich. The reasoning behind the effects of inequality on human development can be twofold. First, such income inequality can induce inequalities in human development because in more unequal societies, less people can afford to live a healthy life and to spend their money on education. This effect should even be higher in autocracies where service provision according to our argumentation does not function well. Democratic political systems should compensate the negative effect of income inequality. The higher the income inequality, the larger the distance of the median voter's income to the average income. Following the median voter hypothesis, more redistribution will be demanded. Thus, along with a higher income inequality, the redistribution effect of democracy increases. Public service provision will be at a higher level that may result in better human development outcomes.

5.2.3 Summary and Working Hypotheses

Summarizing the theoretical arguments above, we can state that democratic regimes in comparison to autocratic ones are expected to produce a higher rate of redistribution and thus to higher public expenditures. Additionally, public spending priorities in democracies reflect the needs of the society more than do the ones in autocracies. Execution of public budgets will be in those sectors where public demand is most obvious. Moreover, democratic control mechanisms will

Besley and Burgess (2002)). The same is supposed to hold for the institutionalization of parties and accountability issues.

[12]The argument that the median voter is farther away from the mean when a society is more unequal is true for right-skewed distributions. This is usually the case for the national income distributions, which are quite close to log-normal distributions.

assure the implementation of policies so that a high degree of compliance with laws, directives and orders is reached. Hence, public action can translate into the desired human development outcomes, for example a better health status of the population or a lower illiteracy rate. But the performance of democracies will vary according to the specific circumstances. We assume that the level of income, education, social fragmentation and the level of income inequality all affect the level of the provision of public goods and human development in a democratic system. Therefore, the following general hypotheses can be derived:

a) Democratic political systems will yield better results in human development than autocracies, independently from the level of economic development.

b) The positive effect of democracies on public goods provision will be intensified by the level of economic development.

c) The positive effect of democracy on human development will be higher, the higher the level of education in a society.

d) Social fragmentation lowers the positive impact of democracies on human development. The more socially diverse a country is the more difficult it is to provide broad-based services even in democracies.

e) The redistribution effect of democracy compensates the negative effect of income inequality on human development. Furthermore, the higher the level of inequality, the bigger the positive effect of democracy on human development.

5.3 Empirical Links between Democracy and Human Development

5.3.1 Empirical Implementation

To quantify human development, we focus on the non-income components of UNDP's Human Development Index and consequently use UNDP's data on life expectancy at birth and on literacy rates. Life expectancy at birth is measured in years, whereas the literacy rate is an index value ranging from 0 to 100. We choose education and health as both aspects are direct determinants of capabilities and as they both influence the freedom to choose any lifestyle. Education as well as health raises productivity and the ability to convert income and resources into the favored way of life (Sen, 2003). The third dimension of human development, namely income, is not of interest for this paper, since detailed literature on the relation between democracy and economic development is already available. Our data on political institutions, especially on democracy, is taken from the Polity IV Project of the Center for International Development and Conflict Management at the University of Maryland. This dataset includes the Polity2 score ranging from 10 (highly democratic) to -10 (highly autocratic), while a zero score indicates a state between autocracy and democracy which we consider as not being democratic.[13] Following Besley and Kudamatsu (2006), we take the fraction of democratic years over the past five years as our measure for democracy (demexp). As an alternative measure for democracy we calculate the average Polity2 score over the past five years (mpol). The consideration of a period of five years captures the effect of democratic experience and reduces the uncertainty concerning the length of the delay until a change in the political system affects human development. Another reason for the five year period is that the values of life expectancy and literacy are not updated annually but roughly every five years. Nevertheless, one might argue that it is certainly arbitrary to take five years and not ten, but with this choice, we proxy election periods, we are in line with the existing literature (Besley and Kudamatsu, 2006) and our study is therefore comparable. Having different democracy measures is rather important as a check of robustness.

Other variables we expect to have an impact on human development or that describe possible conditions under which democracy affects human development are the following: GDP per capita PPP in constant prices[14] from the Penn World Tables 6.2; Gini coefficients[15] from the WIDER dataset with improvements in terms of comparability across countries and time by Grün and Klasen (2008); a measure of ethnic fractionalization[16] as proxy for social fragmentation from Alesina et al. (2003) which is constant over time[17]. Since education is also a factor influencing the performance of democracy, literacy rates are also used as an explanatory variable in our panel analysis for life expectancy but neglected in the analysis of literacy itself. As our additional control variables we consider as most important whether a country experienced some conflict in the period under observation and whether a high percentage of population is suffering from HIV/AIDS. To measure war, we take data from the UCDP/PRIO intrastate conflict onset dataset, 1946-2006. We choose the variable warinci2 that measures the incidence of intrastate war and is coded 1 in all country years with at least one active war.[18] For HIV/AIDS, we take adult (15-49 years) HIV prevalence rates from the 2008 Report on the global AIDS epidemic from UNAIDS/WHO. Data coverage over time and countries lead us to the decision to create a variable that takes the value 1 when a country has a prevalence rate over 5 per cent in the year 2003. To

[13] According to the Polity2 measure, a system can be classified as democratic if three interdependent elements exist: 1) competitiveness of participation, institutions and procedures allow citizens to express their political preferences; 2) openness and competitiveness of executive recruitment and constraints on the chief executive, so that the executive power is institutionally constraint; 3) civil liberties. The last element as well as rule of law, system of checks and balances, freedom of the press etc. is not coded in the index as the latter are performance indicators of democratic regimes. Autocracies are defined vice versa.

[14] US$, base year: 2000.

[15] Gini coefficients are not available for every year. We therefore use a simple moving average between available observations to complete the dataset.

[16] The ethnic fractionalization measure renders the probability that two individuals selected at random from a population are members of different groups. It is calculated with data on language and race using the following formula $FRAC_j = 1 - \sum_{i=1}^{N} s_{ij}^2$, where s_{ij} is the proportion of group $i = 1, \dots, N$ in country j going from complete homogeneity (an index of 0) to complete heterogeneity (an index of 1). For more details see Alesina et al. (2003).

[17] According to Alesina et al. (2003) the assumption of stable group shares is not a problem as examples of changes in ethnic fractionalization are rare. At least over the time-horizon of 20 to 30 years, time persistence can be assumed.

[18] War is defined by more than 1000 battle deaths. As intrastate wars are more frequent than interstate wars, we decided to take the intrastate war variable.

take the heterogeneity between autocracies into account we introduce a simple socialism dummy to represent autocracies with a commitment to universal welfare. The dummy takes the value one for all Eastern European countries until 1990, Vietnam until 1980, China until 1975, and for Cuba and North Korea until today.

Unfortunately, the available data on public expenditures were not sufficient for our purposes. Such data would have enriched our analysis as we could have examined the channels that democracy takes to affect human development. We suspect that democracy causes different priorities in public expenditures compared to autocracies. Therefore, increases in public expenditures on health and education can be decomposed into two components: an increase due to higher total expenditures and an increase due to different priorities in government spending. While the first source is mainly driven by economic growth, we expect democracy to be a main driver of the second source. As mentioned above, we were unable to gather sound data for relative government spending for the given period. Only for the more recent years does the Government Finance Statistics of the IMF include sufficient information concerning these issues. Thus, neither the public expenditures' path of causation nor the channel of private spending can be investigated here due to data restrictions. We must therefore rely on the theoretical argumentation that underpins our empirical analysis.

5.3.2 Descriptive Statistics

First, it is worthwhile to take a look at the densities of life expectancy and literacy for democracies and autocracies separately (Figures 5.1 and 5.2). We use kernel density estimators for this purpose and apply boundary corrections at 0 and 100 for the literacy rate and at the minimum and maximum values for life expectancy. While in democracies, both for life expectancy and literacy the mass of the distribution tends to the right hand side, there seems to be a group of autocracies with a low level and another one with a high level of life expectancy and literacy each. The same pattern can be observed in Tables E.1 to E.8 where we classified countries according to three categories: low, middle and high income; autocracy and democracy; low, middle and high life expectancy or literacy rates.[19] On average, we observe that democracies have a higher life expectancy and a higher literacy rate than autocracies. Exceptions are democracies with low life expectancies, mainly due to the HIV/AIDS tragedy in big parts of Sub-Saharan Africa. Considering the rich group of autocracies especially in 2000, it is striking that virtually all of them are oil states. This indicates, at least to some extent, that autocracies have problems catching up with the top of the income distribution, as long as they do not control a large amount of such an important resource as oil. But what is more important for our study is the fact that although these countries show a high level of income, whether caused by natural resources or not, they display lower life expectancies and lower literacy rates than their democratic counterparts.

[19]To define the groups of low, middle and high life expectancy or literacy rates we computed quantiles of life expectancy and literacy. The income groups are defined according to Essay 2.

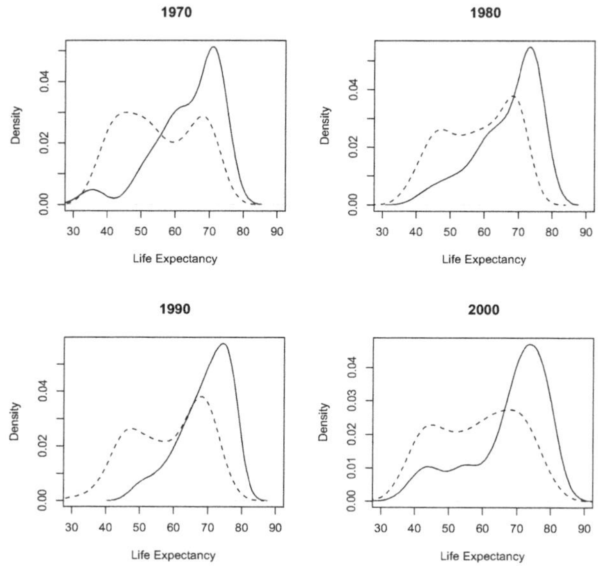

Figure 5.1: Cross-country distribution of life expectancy. Solid line: Kernel density estimator for countries being democratic in the given year. Dashed line: Kernel density estimator for countries being autocratic in the given year. 1970: 41 democracies and 97 autocracies; 1980: 44 democracies and 107 autocracies; 1990: 67 democracies and 85 autocracies; 2000: 97 democracies and 58 autocracies.

5.3.3 Panel Analysis

In a simple model, we try to explain life expectancy and literacy with our measures of democracy controlling for GDP. GDP is lagged for one period to reduce the apparent problem of endogeneity. Additionally to the measuring of democracy and economic development, we include the literacy rate as a proxy of the population's ability to articulate their needs in the political arena, to control politicians' activities and as a proxy of the population's priority for private spending on education and health. We also lag literacy for one period to reduce endogeneity problems. We only include education and its interaction with democracy in the model with life expectancy as our dependent variable. In line with our theoretical reasoning, we incorporate the lagged Gini coefficient to measure the effect of income inequality and ethnic fractionalization as a proxy for social fragmentation.

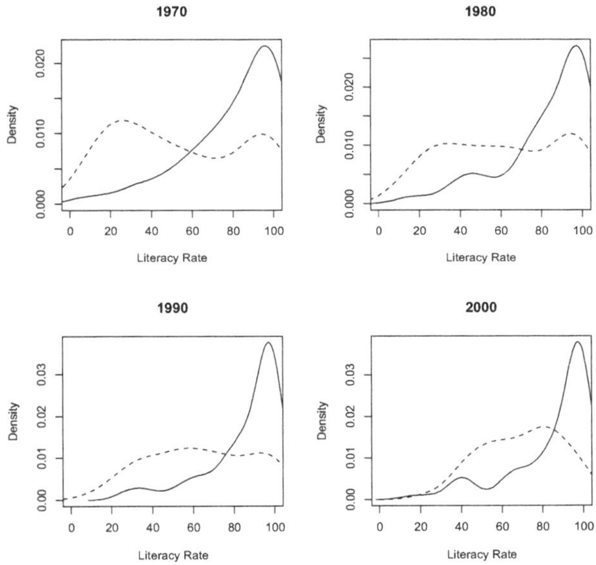

Figure 5.2: Cross-country distribution of literacy rates. Solid line: Kernel density estimator for countries being democratic in the given year. Dashed line: Kernel density estimator for countries being autocratic in the given year. 1970: 23 democracies and 77 autocracies; 1980: 25 democracies and 87 autocracies; 1990: 44 democracies and 68 autocracies; 2000: 70 democracies and 45 autocracies.

As pointed out, all variables describe conditions which potentially hamper or foster the functioning of democracy in terms of addressing the needs of the population. Thus, we are interested in their interaction with democracy on the one hand. On the other hand, we want to know whether they have an effect on human development independently from the political system. Following Cronbach (1987)[20], we center the variables which are used for the modeling of the interaction terms over the cross-section to deal with problems of multicollinearity.

Furthermore, we add a set of dummies for global regions[21] as well as year dummies to all regression. The region dummies should capture much of the geographical, political and historical heterogeneity across the world. The inclusion of period effects allows us to capture overall upward trends in literacy and life expectancy that for example could be explained by technological

[20]See also Jaccard et al. (1990).

[21]Following the World Bank definition.

Table 5.1: Panel analysis for all countries (dependent variable: life expectancy)

	DEMEXP				MPOL			
Democracy	1.238***	1.112***	0.891***	0.845***	0.089***	0.101***	0.067***	0.069***
	(0.136)	(0.169)	(0.139)	(0.145)	(0.010)	(0.011)	(0.010)	(0.010)
GDP(-1)	4.140***	3.982***	3.585***	3.601***	3.813***	3.803***	3.544***	3.867***
	(0.121)	(0.165)	(0.118)	(0.161)	(0.145)	(0.135)	(0.144)	(0.114)
Gini(-1)	0.878	1.185	-0.696	0.019	1.155	1.065	-0.143	-0.178
	(0.719)	(0.775)	(0.499)	(0.715)	(0.716)	(0.597)	(0.694)	(0.599)
Literacy (-1)	0.199***	0.204***	0.214***	0.210***	0.205***	0.202***	0.215***	0.201***
	(0.007)	(0.008)	(0.008)	(0.008)	(0.008)	(0.008)	(0.008)	(0.008)
Fractionalization	-2.100***	-2.474***	-2.233***	-2.801***	-1.919***	-2.407***	-1.895***	-2.450***
	(0.420)	(0.543)	(0.509)	(0.531)	(0.461)	(0.493)	(0.512)	(0.484)
War	-0.635***	-0.644***	-0.691***	-0.675***	-0.651***	-0.543***	-0.825***	-0.566***
	(0.163)	(0.165)	(0.163)	(0.162)	(0.158)	(0.154)	(0.141)	(0.156)
Socialism	2.236***	2.039***			2.197***	2.370***		
	(0.600)	(0.580)			(0.562)	(0.552)		
Aids*1975	0.240	0.192	0.305	-0.187	0.605	0.559	0.619	0.264
	(0.599)	(0.618)	(0.601)	(0.633)	(0.575)	(0.617)	(0.590)	(0.644)
Aids*1980	0.420	0.362	0.445	0.050	0.763	0.759	0.770	0.533
	(0.601)	(0.623)	(0.606)	(0.633)	(0.580)	(0.625)	(0.596)	(0.647)
Aids*1985	0.064	-0.012	-0.012	-0.285	0.312	0.295	0.263	0.125
	(0.616)	(0.642)	(0.622)	(0.646)	(0.598)	(0.645)	(0.615)	(0.660)
Aids*1990	-2.362***	-2.421***	-2.554***	-2.603***	-2.261***	-2.180**	-2.371***	-2.235**
	(0.652)	(0.686)	(0.661)	(0.683)	(0.638)	(0.690)	(0.656)	(0.698)
Aids*1995	-8.044***	-8.128***	-8.376***	-8.535***	-8.116***	-8.067***	-8.249***	-8.205***
	(0.701)	(0.727)	(0.715)	(0.724)	(0.693)	(0.740)	(0.712)	(0.749)
Aids*2000	-15.595***	-15.681***	-15.786***	-16.031***	-15.749***	-15.566***	-15.704***	-15.554***
	(0.776)	(0.812)	(0.795)	(0.800)	(0.777)	(0.839)	(0.795)	(0.837)
Year 1980	0.838***	0.826***	0.859***	0.832***	0.822***	0.808***	0.840***	0.798***
	(0.066)	(0.062)	(0.069)	(0.058)	(0.065)	(0.068)	(0.069)	(0.064)
Year 1985	1.897***	1.845***	1.889***	1.849***	1.861***	1.809***	1.871***	1.825***
	(0.088)	(0.084)	(0.094)	(0.078)	(0.088)	(0.090)	(0.093)	(0.087)
Year 1990	2.374***	2.304***	2.412***	2.347***	2.355***	2.244***	2.393***	2.293***
	(0.103)	(0.099)	(0.111)	(0.093)	(0.103)	(0.104)	(0.110)	(0.102)
Year 1995	2.908***	2.823***	2.968***	2.830***	2.894***	2.715***	2.939***	2.752***
	(0.115)	(0.109)	(0.124)	(0.100)	(0.117)	(0.111)	(0.126)	(0.111)
Year 2000	3.332***	3.251***	3.355***	3.258***	3.316***	3.169***	3.290***	3.169***
	(0.127)	(0.123)	(0.140)	(0.111)	(0.131)	(0.119)	(0.138)	(0.117)
Dem.*GDP		-0.132		-0.073		0.037*		0.039*
		(0.265)		(0.254)		(0.017)		(0.016)
Dem.*Literacy		-0.008		-0.013		-0.001*		-0.002***
		(0.009)		(0.010)		(0.001)		(0.001)
Dem.*Gini		2.251		5.682***		0.270**		0.450***
		(1.412)		(1.295)		(0.088)		(0.070)
Dem.*Fract.		-2.674***		-2.526***		-0.142**		-0.136**
		(0.762)		(0.711)		(0.050)		(0.050)
constant	60.442***	60.687***	61.129***	61.235***	60.758***	60.412***	61.260***	60.803***
	(0.200)	(0.228)	(0.233)	(0.229)	(0.224)	(0.220)	(0.236)	(0.218)
N	621	621	621	621	621	621	621	621

* p<0.05, ** p<0.01, *** p<0.001; dummies for global regions included and jointly signifficant

improvements (Pritchett and Summers 1996). Moreover, we control in both regressions for war, because it destroys lives as well as infrastructure that would otherwise provide health and education services. Additionally, we control for HIV/AIDS in the life expectancy regressions. The AIDS dummy variable is interacted with the year dummies because HIV/AIDS was more of a

Table 5.2: Panel analysis for non-OECD countries (dependent variable: life expectancy)

	DEMEXP				MPOL			
Democracy	1.159***	1.202***	1.075***	0.934***	0.078***	0.098***	0.073***	0.066***
	(0.166)	(0.205)	(0.153)	(0.186)	(0.012)	(0.016)	(0.012)	(0.014)
GDP(-1)	3.334***	3.339***	3.738***	3.438***	3.304***	3.495***	3.580***	3.594***
	(0.214)	(0.227)	(0.115)	(0.194)	(0.206)	(0.194)	(0.134)	(0.165)
Gini(-1)	-0.785	0.098	-1.926**	-0.935	-0.683	0.859	-1.342**	-0.040
	(0.820)	(0.893)	(0.603)	(0.942)	(0.855)	(0.888)	(0.489)	(0.782)
Literacy (-1)	0.203***	0.198***	0.197***	0.196***	0.194***	0.190***	0.195***	0.190***
	(0.009)	(0.010)	(0.009)	(0.009)	(0.009)	(0.010)	(0.009)	(0.010)
Fractionalization	-1.708*	-3.379***	-2.078**	-3.757***	-2.632***	-3.161***	-2.029**	-3.396***
	(0.745)	(0.725)	(0.668)	(0.692)	(0.785)	(0.801)	(0.668)	(0.743)
War	-0.797***	-0.786***	-0.831***	-0.745***	-0.903***	-0.779***	-0.991***	-0.702***
	(0.159)	(0.165)	(0.164)	(0.167)	(0.128)	(0.172)	(0.130)	(0.169)
Socialism	5.057***	4.985***			4.970***	5.229***		
	(0.831)	(0.853)			(0.852)	(0.890)		
Aids*1975	0.932	0.657	0.938	0.209	1.359*	1.070	1.258*	0.672
	(0.664)	(0.675)	(0.640)	(0.681)	(0.635)	(0.668)	(0.625)	(0.679)
Aids*1980	0.828	0.563	0.955	0.276	1.315*	0.964	1.314*	0.724
	(0.665)	(0.680)	(0.643)	(0.680)	(0.639)	(0.677)	(0.630)	(0.684)
Aids*1985	0.164	-0.076	0.421	-0.203	0.613	0.215	0.706	0.099
	(0.677)	(0.695)	(0.656)	(0.690)	(0.656)	(0.697)	(0.646)	(0.698)
Aids*1990	-2.477***	-2.586***	-2.124**	-2.570***	-2.086**	-2.426**	-1.920**	-2.399**
	(0.709)	(0.732)	(0.690)	(0.721)	(0.692)	(0.739)	(0.683)	(0.735)
Aids*1995	-8.181***	-8.200***	-7.670***	-8.204***	-7.804***	-8.031***	-7.506***	-8.055***
	(0.760)	(0.776)	(0.744)	(0.761)	(0.748)	(0.788)	(0.741)	(0.781)
Aids*2000	-15.401***	-15.481***	-14.983***	-15.576***	-15.138***	-15.319***	-14.882***	-15.250***
	(0.830)	(0.854)	(0.822)	(0.834)	(0.826)	(0.885)	(0.828)	(0.870)
Year 1980	1.186***	1.200***	1.113***	1.103***	1.172***	1.214***	1.086***	1.091***
	(0.115)	(0.121)	(0.115)	(0.116)	(0.116)	(0.123)	(0.116)	(0.117)
Year 1985	2.476***	2.507***	2.356***	2.361***	2.509***	2.582***	2.361***	2.395***
	(0.158)	(0.164)	(0.159)	(0.158)	(0.159)	(0.170)	(0.161)	(0.161)
Year 1990	3.195***	3.163***	3.031***	3.009***	3.247***	3.252***	3.042***	3.048***
	(0.192)	(0.197)	(0.194)	(0.192)	(0.193)	(0.205)	(0.196)	(0.196)
Year 1995	3.606***	3.542***	3.369***	3.318***	3.648***	3.615***	3.369***	3.353***
	(0.224)	(0.229)	(0.227)	(0.224)	(0.226)	(0.240)	(0.229)	(0.228)
Year 2000	3.880***	3.849***	3.715***	3.711***	4.009***	3.965***	3.760***	3.721***
	(0.240)	(0.244)	(0.233)	(0.241)	(0.242)	(0.252)	(0.231)	(0.236)
Dem.*GDP		-0.329		-0.381		0.003		0.015
		(0.288)		(0.279)		(0.020)		(0.019)
Dem.*Literacy		-0.002		-0.009		-0.000		-0.002*
		(0.010)		(0.010)		(0.001)		(0.001)
Dem.*Gini		2.377		4.354**		0.091		0.290*
		(1.612)		(1.659)		(0.116)		(0.123)
Dem.*Fract.		-3.057**		-3.166***		-0.146		-0.139
		(0.968)		(0.925)		(0.076)		(0.075)
constant	58.833***	59.052***	59.576***	60.221***	59.674***	59.194***	59.879***	60.407***
	(0.325)	(0.326)	(0.219)	(0.337)	(0.323)	(0.344)	(0.224)	(0.320)
N	469	469	469	469	469	469	469	469

* p<0.05, ** p<0.01, *** p<0.001; dummies for global regions included and jointly signifficant

problem for the more recent years in the sample and less in the earlier ones. A socialism dummy aims to capture heterogeneity across autocracies and an egalitarian tendency in those regimes.

We estimate the model for the years 1970, 1975, 1980, 1985, 1990, 1995 and 2000 (and the preceding five year periods), as both literacy rate and life expectancy are not updated annually but roughly every five years, while being interpolated in the other years. Pre-estimation diagnostics

Table 5.3: Panel analysis for non-OECD countries (dependent variable: literacy rate)

	DEMEXP				MPOL			
Democracy	1.643***	1.169**	1.261***	1.691***	0.300***	0.055	0.081**	0.059*
	(0.374)	(0.414)	(0.329)	(0.420)	(0.018)	(0.036)	(0.026)	(0.026)
GDP(-1)	11.685***	10.358***	11.101***	10.320***	11.499***	11.098***	11.645***	11.260***
	(0.451)	(0.494)	(0.453)	(0.502)	(0.471)	(0.498)	(0.441)	(0.441)
Gini(-1)	5.010**	-5.292**	-2.277	-4.329	6.463**	-1.452	-0.991	-2.428
	(1.570)	(1.828)	(1.980)	(2.246)	(2.379)	(1.970)	(2.164)	(1.566)
Fractionalization	-8.857***	-8.748***	-12.101***	-12.087***	-3.516**	-10.025***	-11.158***	-12.723***
	(1.695)	(1.903)	(1.617)	(2.074)	(1.338)	(2.103)	(1.594)	(1.817)
Socialism	8.627***	6.947**			10.897***	7.046**		
	(2.237)	(2.283)			(2.175)	(2.255)		
War	0.221	-0.311	-0.017	-0.304	-0.581*	-0.060	-0.015	-0.099
	(0.350)	(0.351)	(0.350)	(0.330)	(0.232)	(0.369)	(0.372)	(0.380)
Year 1980	2.896***	2.917***	2.806***	2.917***	3.033***	2.843***	2.799***	2.761***
	(0.293)	(0.286)	(0.276)	(0.284)	(0.316)	(0.286)	(0.274)	(0.278)
Year 1985	6.613***	6.724***	6.396***	6.620***	6.611***	6.649***	6.463***	6.515***
	(0.393)	(0.385)	(0.369)	(0.382)	(0.422)	(0.385)	(0.364)	(0.375)
Year 1990	9.384***	9.618***	9.229***	9.455***	9.316***	9.437***	9.261***	9.359***
	(0.469)	(0.465)	(0.440)	(0.462)	(0.502)	(0.464)	(0.434)	(0.449)
Year 1995	11.841***	12.214***	11.633***	11.928***	11.031***	11.871***	11.624***	11.633***
	(0.550)	(0.541)	(0.515)	(0.542)	(0.580)	(0.540)	(0.511)	(0.520)
Year 2000	13.861***	14.185***	13.878***	13.801***	12.857***	13.890***	13.643***	13.647***
	(0.563)	(0.552)	(0.525)	(0.573)	(0.580)	(0.557)	(0.506)	(0.519)
Dem.*GDP		-0.935*		-0.250		-0.074		-0.065*
		(0.466)		(0.492)		(0.038)		(0.033)
Dem.*Fract.		0.867		1.988		0.106		0.129
		(1.765)		(1.741)		(0.144)		(0.133)
Dem.*Gini		-10.606***		-10.646***		-0.451		-0.173
		(2.846)		(3.064)		(0.232)		(0.185)
_cons	81.373***	81.681***	82.580***	79.570***	81.667***	82.503***	83.806***	82.878***
	(0.699)	(0.589)	(0.564)	(0.710)	(0.615)	(0.773)	(0.518)	(0.572)
N	526	526	526	526	526	526	526	526

* p<0.05, ** p<0.01, *** p<0.001; dummies for global regions included and jointly signifficant

indicate that heteroscedasticity and autocorrelation have to be dealt with. We therefore find the estimation of our model with a cross-sectional time-series FGLS regression with panel specific AR(1) to be the most appropriate, addressing both issues simultaneously (stata command: xtgls). In case of life expectancy, we run separate regressions for non-OECD countries and the entire sample. For literacy, only the regression for the sub-sample of non-OECD makes sense as all OECD countries have a constant level of literacy of exactly 99 percent in the UNDP data. The results are presented in Tables 5.1 to 5.3.

The results for the control variables are as expected in all specifications. The coefficients of the year dummies are positive and highly significant for all years. The numbers are continuously increasing over time and are thus capturing overall progress for human development due to for instance technology. The AIDS*time dummies are negative and highly significant for 1990, 1995 and 2000. This result displays the tragedy of HIV/AIDS and its immense impact on life expectancy in many African countries during this period. The coefficient of the War dummy is highly negative significant in the regressions with life expectancy as dependent variable and insignificant in the regressions with the literacy rate as dependent variable. The coefficient of the socialism dummy is positive and highly significant whenever included.

There is a strong positive and highly significant correlation between our measures of human development and democracy in merely all specifications (we will discuss the one exception below). The coefficients of the other main explanatory variables carry the expected signs and are highly significant, except for the Gini variable, which has an insignificant sign in most cases. The coefficient of GDP per capita is positive, the literacy rate has a positive coefficient in the life expectancy regressions (remember that it is not included in the regressions where literacy is the dependent variable), and fractionalization carries a negative sign. All these results are robust to the choice of the democracy measure; they hold both for the fraction of democratic years (demexp) and the average Polity2 score (mpol).
When it comes to the interaction effects of democracy with GDP per capita, ethnic fractionalization, inequality and literacy respectively the results are rather ambiguous. The interaction of GDP and democracy sometimes carries a positive sign and sometimes a negative sign depending on the measure of democracy and the countries included in the sample. In fact, it is insignificant in most cases. We conclude that there is no robust evidence for this interaction and thus the democracy's performance seems to not depend on the level of economic development. A similar argument holds true for the interaction of inequality and democracy. It is positive and significant in the life expectancy regressions when the socialism dummy is not included and it is not significant when the socialism dummy is included. Thus, its effect is fully captured by the socialism dummy[22] In the literacy regression, the Gini interaction effect is only significant for one of the two democracy measures (demexp) and thus not fully reliable. Contrary to the median voter prediction, it carries a negative sign in this case. The interaction of democracy and literacy is only significant for mpol and not for demexp. The interaction of democracy and ethnic fractionalization is significant in the life expectancy regressions for the full sample; it carries the expected negative sign. For the sample of non-OECD countries, it is only significant when demexp is used as measure of democracy, both for literacy and life expectancy. Hence, there is more support for this interaction effect in the data than for the others, but it is still rather weak and not robust to different measures.
Overall, there is only weak evidence for any of these interactions. The specifications excluding interaction effects are therefore the more valid and reliable ones. This might also explain why there is no significant effect of democracy on literacy in the model including mpol and all interaction effects. Summarizing, it can be said that a democracy's influence on life expectancy and literacy is positive and robust but does not depend on the circumstances.

5.4 Conclusions

We believe that our study has its associated merits explaining the linkage between democracy and human development. In our theoretical section, we clarified the causal channels of democracy influencing human development. In contrast to earlier studies, which put their focus on property rights, we emphasized the importance of the redistributive effects and effects of public goods provision in democracy. The influence of democracy on human development is investigated

[22]Indeed, inequality is higher in socialist autocracies with a higher life expectancy and literacy than in other autocracies.

descriptively and analytically, the statistical analysis includes both the cross-sectional and the time dimension. Extending existing literature, we not only measure the influence of democracy on human development, but we theoretically and empirically analyze conditions that are assumed to be important for the functioning of democracy in terms of improving the level of human development.

Empirically, we have been able to show that there is a strong and robust correlation between democracy and human development measured by life expectancy at birth and the literacy rate, even if controlling for the level of economic development and other important variables. Thus, it seems to be the political system that makes a difference for the population's well-being. Relying both on theoretical reasoning as well as careful empirical implementation, we are convinced that this is also a causal relationship, although we have to admit that the results give evidence for but do not definitely prove this claim.

However, we can be less certain that the influence comes directly from a democratic system. Question remains whether it is driven by other social and political factors, which are very well proxied by democracy. Against the background of democracy, other factors might be at work as well. Future studies could incorporate social capital as well as the degree of decentralization of the political-administrative system. In addition, it would certainly be an improvement of our analysis to empirically identify and model the channels that democracy takes before it affects human development, for example via the public expenditures. Unfortunately, the data for this endeavor have not been available.

Theoretical expectations about the concise conditions interacting with democracy in the creation of a healthy and literate society have not been met. We found only very little evidence for conditions and requirements that increase or decrease the impact of democracy on human development. The interaction of democracy and its other presumed conditions of functioning turned out to be insignificant or not robust to different democracy measures or samples. One could therefore conclude that the functioning of democracy - in terms of non-income human development improvements - is rather independent of GDP per capita, inequality, education and also ethnic fractionalization. The missing robustness of our interaction effects does not permit any inferences.

Nevertheless, GDP per capita, education and ethnic fractionalization influence non-income human development levels directly. A high level of economic development and education is related to a high level of non-income human development. High social fragmentation, on the contrary, leads to lower levels of non-income human development. Income inequality has rather ambiguous results and turns out to be insignificant in most cases.

To sum up: It is democracy itself that is important and to a smaller extent the circumstances under which it occurs. This stands in contrast to what theoretical literature has told us. However, it can be considered as good news for promoting democracy in poor, fragmented or uneducated societies.

To sum up, we can derive two main conclusions from our analysis. First, democracy is good for human development, independently from the level of economic development in a country. Second, even if the picture here is more ambiguous, the positive impact of democracy on human development seems to be rather independent from the circumstances. Since income inequality did not play a major role in our estimations we found no supporting evidence for the median voter theory. Nevertheless, as democracy positively affects the well-being of a population, the main question of this paper deserves an affirmative answer. We thus cautiously support Sen's argument stating that democracy fulfils its "constructive" and "instrumental" role.

Appendix to Essay 1

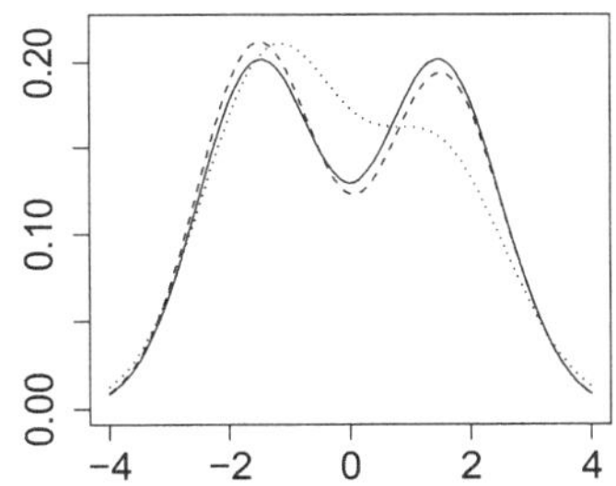

Figure A.1: Density of normal mixture $f_1(x) = f(x, 0.5, -1.5, 1.5, 1, 1)$ (solid line), together with unrestricted fit to sample of size 500 from f_1 (dashed line) and restricted unimodal fit (dotted line).

Table A.1: Model selection criteria for mixture models fitted to the cross-sectional log-income distribution of European regions

comp.	variances	no. param.	AIC 1977	BIC 1977	AIC 1990	BIC 1990
1	-	2	-131.70	-126.39	-133.96	-128.66
2	equal	4	-160.99	-150.38	- 145.47	-134.85
	distinct	5	-159.56	-146.29	-144.26	-130.97
3	equal	6	-156.99	-141.07	-141.47	-125.55
	distinct	8	-154.09	-132.86	-144.14	-122.91

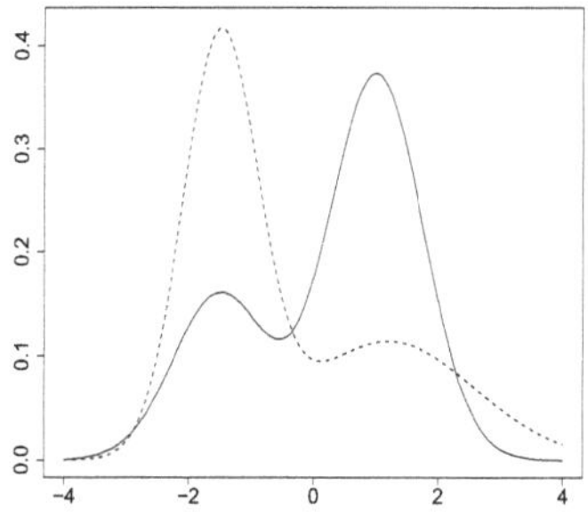

Figure A.2: Densities of normal mixtures $f_2(x) = f(x, 0.3, -1.5, 1, 0.75, 0.75)$ (solid line) and $f_3(x) = f(x, 0.6, -1.5, 1.4, 0.6, 1.4)$ (dashed line).

Appendix to Essay 2

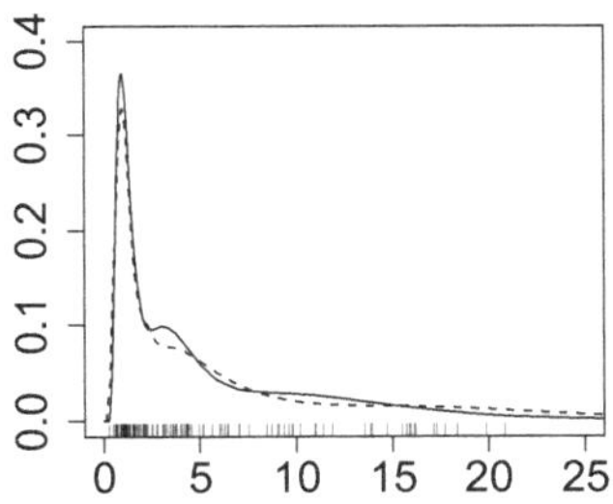

Figure B.1: Three-component mixture density with equal variances (solid line) and transformation kernel density estimate based on $h_c(3)$ for 1976. Scale: x-axix 10^3, y-axis 10^{-3}.

Table B.1: Model selection criteria for mixtures models fitted to log cross-country income distribution, 1976

no. components	- loglike.	no. param.	AIC	BIC
1	77.86	2	159.72	165.41
2	70.86	4	149.72	161.10
3	66.90	6	145.80	162.87

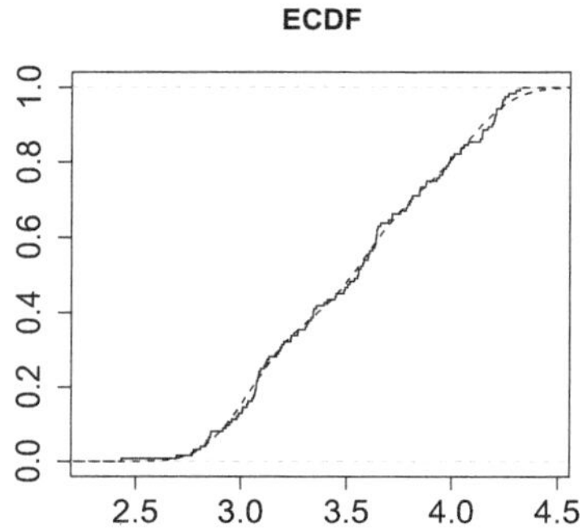

Figure B.2: Empirical cumulative distribution function (cdf) for the log-data (logarithm to the base 10) for 1976 (solid line) and cdf of the three-component normal mixture with equal variances (dashed line).

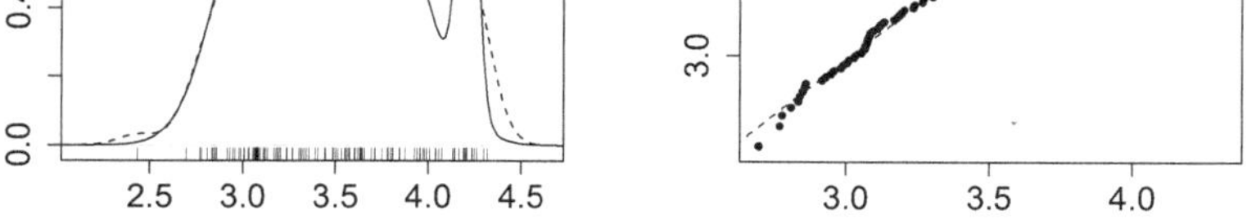

Figure B.3: Left: Three-component mixture density with distinct variances (solid line) and kernel density estimate based on $h_c(3)$ (dashed line) for the log-data (logarithm to the base 10) for 1976. Right: QQ-Plot of the log-data for 1976 against the quantiles of the normal mixture (three components, distinct variances) together with least squares fit (dashed line).

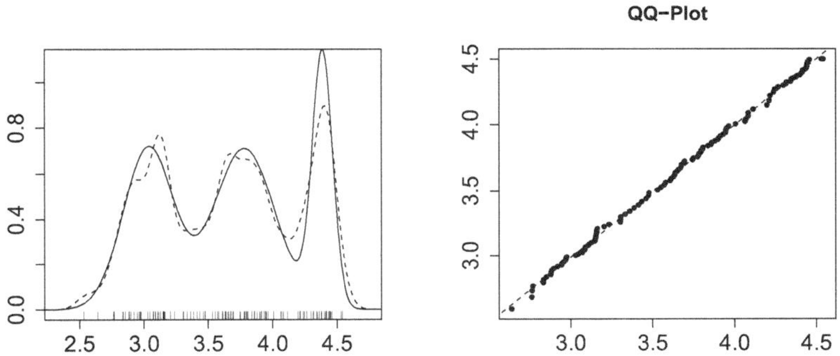

Figure B.4: Left: Three-component mixture density with distinct variances (solid line) and kernel density estimate based on $h_c(3)$ (dashed line) for the log-data (logarithm to the base 10) for 2003. Right: QQ-Plot of the log-data for 2003 against the quantiles of the normal mixture (three components, distinct variances) together with least squares fit (dashed line).

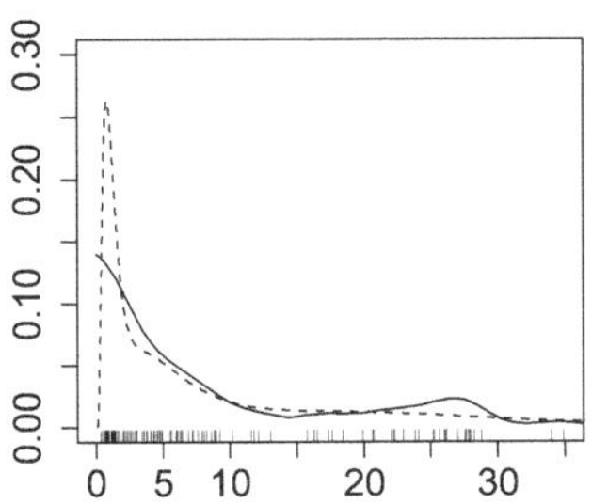

Figure B.5: Kernel density estimate (solid line) and transformation kernel density estimate (dashed line) with log-transform, both with bandwidth estimated by direct plug-in, for 2003. Scale: x-axis 10^3, y-axis 10^{-3}.

Table B.2: Results of Silverman's test for 2003, 124 countries

	$h_c(1)$	p_1	$h_c(2)$	p_2	$h_c(3)$	p_3
y_i's	0.27	0.11	0.23	0.00	0.07	0.91
x_i's	5.72	0.01	2.14	0.44	1.83	0.24

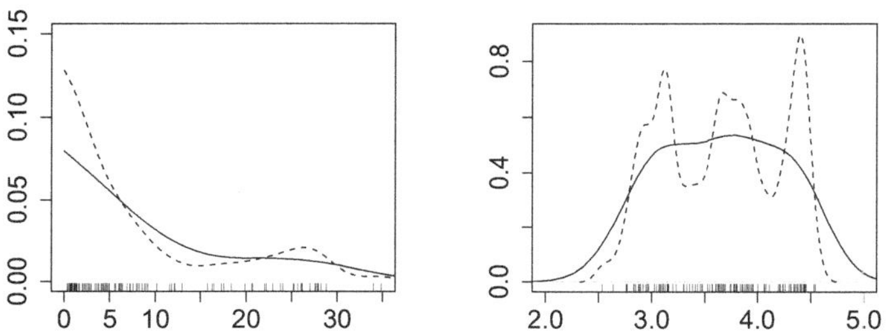

Figure B.6: Left: Kernel density estimates with boundary correction at zero with bandwidths $h_c(1)$ (solid line) and $h_c(2)$ (dashed line) for the cross-country income distribution in 2003. Scale: x-axis 10^3, y-axis: 10^{-3}. Right: Kernel density estimates with bandwidths $h_c(1)$ (solid line) and $h_c(3)$ (dashed line) for the log-income distribution in 2003. For conveniently interpreting the figure, we here use the logarithm to the base 10.

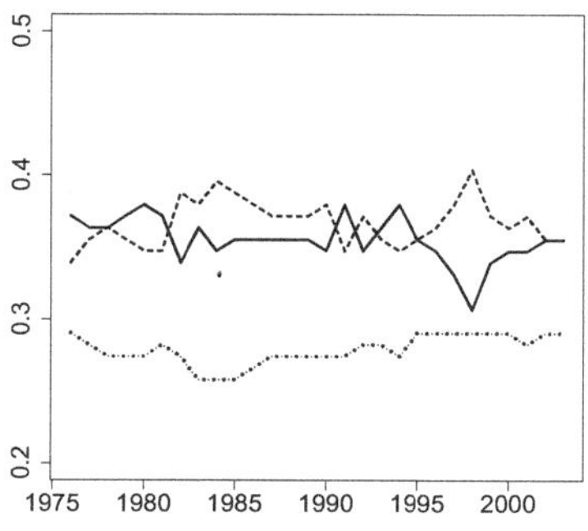

Figure B.7: Weights of mixture components. Poor (solid line), intermediate (dashed line) and rich component (dotted line).

Table B.3: Fit of the three-component model

Year	p_1	p_2	p_3	μ_1	μ_2	μ_3	σ	Mean1	Mean2	Mean3	SE 1	SE 2	SE 3
1976	0.379	0.338	0.284	3.044	3.587	4.076	0.175	1147	3998	12335	310	1082	3337
1980	0.366	0.351	0.282	3.041	3.622	4.115	0.177	1141	4342	13526	313	1191	3710
1985	0.358	0.372	0.270	3.035	3.639	4.154	0.181	1126	4524	14806	316	1268	4149
1990	0.357	0.367	0.276	3.041	3.649	4.211	0.182	1140	4628	16887	320	1299	4741
1995	0.355	0.364	0.281	2.996	3.665	4.247	0.189	1032	4813	18396	303	1413	5400
2000	0.345	0.371	0.284	3.017	3.698	4.313	0.177	1079	5174	21312	295	1415	5830
2003	0.357	0.353	0.290	3.037	3.725	4.326	0.176	1128	5504	21938	307	1496	5962

Table B.4: Posterior means, 1976 and 2003

Land	Posterior Mean 1976	Rank 1976	Posterior Mean 2003	Rank 2003	Change Posterior Mean	Group 1976 and 2003
China	1	115	2	60	1	1 to 2
Korea Republic of	1.999	60	2.984	27	0.985	2 to 3
Taiwan	2.041	47	2.994	25	0.953	2 to 3
Sri Lanka	1.087	87	1.996	66	0.909	1 to 2
India	1.014	97	1.891	76	0.877	1 to 2
Equatorial Guinea	1.787	72	2.639	36	0.852	2 to 3
Cyprus	2.195	42	2.997	22	0.802	2 to 3
Malaysia	2.018	55	2.723	34	0.705	2 to 3
Indonesia	1.291	81	1.994	69	0.703	1 to 2
Pakistan	1.035	90	1.673	79	0.638	1 to 2
Mauritius	2.339	39	2.972	29	0.633	2 to 3
Chile	2.117	43	2.724	33	0.607	2 to 3
Egypt	1.462	79	2	60	0.538	1 to 2
Botswana	1.603	74	2.077	44	0.474	2
Thailand	1.598	75	2.034	47	0.436	2
Cameroon	1.428	80	1.761	78	0.333	1 to 2
Bangladesh	1.024	93	1.255	82	0.231	1
Hungary	2.645	32	2.825	32	0.18	3
Portugal	2.832	30	2.981	28	0.149	3
Lesotho	1.001	112	1.148	85	0.147	1
Ireland	2.87	28	3	1	0.13	3
Swaziland	2.051	46	2.167	39	0.116	2
Hong Kong	2.906	26	3	1	0.094	3
Morocco	1.903	70	1.992	70	0.089	2
Singapore	2.918	24	3	1	0.082	3
Puerto Rico	2.917	25	2.998	19	0.081	3
Panama	2.036	48	2.091	43	0.055	2
Tunisia	2.003	59	2.048	46	0.045	2
Cuba	1.974	65	2.01	52	0.036	2
Dominican Republic	1.988	64	2.022	49	0.034	2
Trinidad + Tobago	2.961	21	2.989	26	0.028	3
Guinea	1.825	71	1.853	77	0.028	2
Philippines	1.951	68	1.977	73	0.026	2
Spain	2.977	19	2.996	23	0.019	3
Japan	2.991	18	2.999	11	0.008	3
Paraguay	1.993	62	2.001	59	0.008	2
Finland	2.992	15	2.999	11	0.007	3

continued on next page

Land	Posterior Mean 1976	Rank 1976	Posterior Mean 2003	Rank 2003	Change Posterior Mean	Group 1976 and 2003
Italy	2.992	15	2.998	19	0.006	3
Nepal	1.001	112	1.007	89	0.006	1
Korea Dem. Rep.	1	115	1.006	92	0.006	1
United Kingdom	2.995	14	2.999	11	0.004	3
Israel	2.992	15	2.996	23	0.004	3
Laos	1.002	111	1.006	92	0.004	1
Austria	2.997	8	3	1	0.003	3
Australia	2.997	8	3	1	0.003	3
Belgium	2.996	13	2.999	11	0.003	3
Mongolia	1.016	95	1.019	87	0.003	1
Norway	2.998	5	3	1	0.002	3
Canada	2.998	5	3	1	0.002	3
Germany	2.997	8	2.999	11	0.002	3
France	2.997	8	2.999	11	0.002	3
United States	2.999	2	3	1	0.001	3
Denmark	2.999	2	3	1	0.001	3
Netherlands	2.998	5	2.999	11	0.001	3
New Zealand	2.997	8	2.998	19	0.001	3
Ghana	1.006	105	1.007	89	0.001	1
Mali	1	115	1.001	100	0.001	1
Switzerland	3	1	3	1	0	3
Sweden	2.999	2	2.999	11	0	3
Tanzania	1	115	1	105	0	1
Malawi	1	115	1	105	0	1
Cambodia	1	115	1	105	0	1
Guinea-Bissau	1	115	1	105	0	1
Ethiopia	1	115	1	105	0	1
Bhutan	1	115	1	105	0	1
Burkina Faso	1	115	1	105	0	1
Oman	2.97	20	2.969	30	-0.001	3
Greece	2.961	21	2.96	31	-0.001	3
Burundi	1.001	112	1	105	-0.001	1
Rwanda	1.006	105	1.003	97	-0.003	1
Uganda	1.004	107	1.001	100	-0.003	1
Chad	1.003	109	1	105	-0.003	1
Gambia	1.003	109	1	105	-0.003	1
Turkey	2.008	58	2.004	57	-0.004	2
Mozambique	1.012	101	1.008	88	-0.004	1
Central African Rep.	1.004	107	1	105	-0.004	1

continued on next page

Land	Posterior Mean 1976	Rank 1976	Posterior Mean 2003	Rank 2003	Change Posterior Mean	Group 1976 and 2003
Guatemala	1.993	62	1.988	71	-0.005	2
Jordan	1.994	61	1.986	72	-0.008	2
Benin	1.013	98	1.004	96	-0.009	1
Kenya	1.01	103	1.001	100	-0.009	1
Niger	1.009	104	1	105	-0.009	1
Madagascar	1.011	102	1	105	-0.011	1
Sudan	1.013	98	1.001	100	-0.012	1
Somalia	1.013	98	1	105	-0.013	1
Congo Dem Rep.	1.015	96	1	105	-0.015	1
Papua New Guinea	2.015	57	1.999	64	-0.016	2
Fiji	2.017	56	2	60	-0.017	2
Nigeria	1.018	94	1.001	100	-0.017	1
Colombia	2.027	54	2.008	54	-0.019	2
Sierra Leone	1.027	92	1	105	-0.027	1
Algeria	2.035	50	2.007	55	-0.028	2
Romania	2.033	52	2.005	56	-0.028	2
Togo	1.03	91	1	105	-0.03	1
El Salvador	2.031	53	2	60	-0.031	2
Jamaica	2.036	48	1.999	64	-0.037	2
Ecuador	2.035	50	1.995	67	-0.04	2
Syria	1.193	83	1.153	84	-0.04	1
Bolivia	1.959	67	1.895	75	-0.064	2
Zambia	1.064	89	1	105	-0.064	1
Mauritania	1.077	88	1.007	89	-0.07	1
Namibia	2.089	45	2.004	57	-0.085	2
Senegal	1.1	86	1.006	92	-0.094	1
Congo Republic of	1.113	85	1.006	92	-0.107	1
Peru	2.114	44	1.995	67	-0.119	2
Honduras	1.503	78	1.384	81	-0.119	2 to 1
Poland	2.387	37	2.205	38	-0.182	2
Liberia	1.184	84	1	105	-0.184	1
Russia	2.861	29	2.672	35	-0.189	3
Mexico	2.298	40	2.068	45	-0.23	2
Brazil	2.274	41	2.031	48	-0.243	2
Costa Rica	2.376	38	2.124	42	-0.252	2
Comoros	1.283	82	1.002	98	-0.281	1
South Africa	2.525	35	2.153	41	-0.372	3 to 2
Uruguay	2.534	34	2.155	40	-0.379	3 to 2
Zimbabwe	1.968	66	1.532	80	-0.436	2

continued on next page

Land	Posterior Mean 1976	Rank 1976	Posterior Mean 2003	Rank 2003	Change Posterior Mean	Group 1976 and 2003
Cote d'Ivoire	1.598	75	1.155	83	-0.443	2 to1
Solomon Islands	1.549	77	1.036	86	-0.513	2 to 1
Nicaragua	2.523	36	1.965	74	-0.558	3 to 2
Argentina	2.937	23	2.371	37	-0.566	3 to 2
Ukraine	2.645	32	2.012	50	-0.633	3 to 2
Afghanistan	1.651	73	1	105	-0.651	2 to1
Iran	2.8	31	2.012	50	-0.788	3 to 2
Venezuela	2.891	27	2.01	52	-0.881	3 to 2
Iraq	1.912	69	1.002	98	-0.91	2 to 1

Appendix to Essay 3

Table C.1: Regions and associated countries

OECD Countries
Australia, Austria, Belgium, Canada, Denmark, Finland, France, Germany, Greece, Ireland, Italy, Japan, Luxembourg, Netherlands, New Zealand, Norway, Portugal, Spain, Sweden, Switzerland, United Kingdom, United States
East Asia and the Pacific
Cambodia, China, Fiji, Hong Kong, Indonesia, Republic of Korea, Laos, Malaysia, Mongolia, Papua New Guinea, Philippines, Singapore, Taiwan, Thailand
Latin America and the Caribbean
Argentina, Bahamas, Barbados, Bolivia, Brazil, Chile, Colombia, Costa Rica, Cuba, Dominican Republic, Ecuador, El Salvador, Guatemala, Honduras, Jamaica, Mexico, Nicaragua, Panama, Paraguay, Peru, Puerto Rico, Suriname, Trinidad and Tobago, Uruguay, Venezuela
Middle East and North Africa
Algeria, Egypt, Iran, Iraq, Israel, Jordan, Morocco, Tunisia
Eastern Europe and Central Asia
Hungary, Poland, Romania, Russia, Turkey, Ukraine
South Asia
Bangladesh, India, Nepal, Pakistan, Sri Lanka
Sub-Saharan Africa
Botswana, Burkina Faso, Burundi, Cameroon, Central African Republic, Chad, Democratic Republic of Congo, Republic of Congo, Cote d'Ivoire, Ethiopia, The Gambia, Ghana, Guinea, Guinea-Bissau, Kenya, Lesotho, Madagascar, Malawi, Mali, Mauritania, Mauritius, Mozambique, Namibia, Niger, Nigeria, Senegal, Sierra Leone, South Africa, Sudan, Swaziland, Tanzani, Uganda, Zambia, Zimbabwe

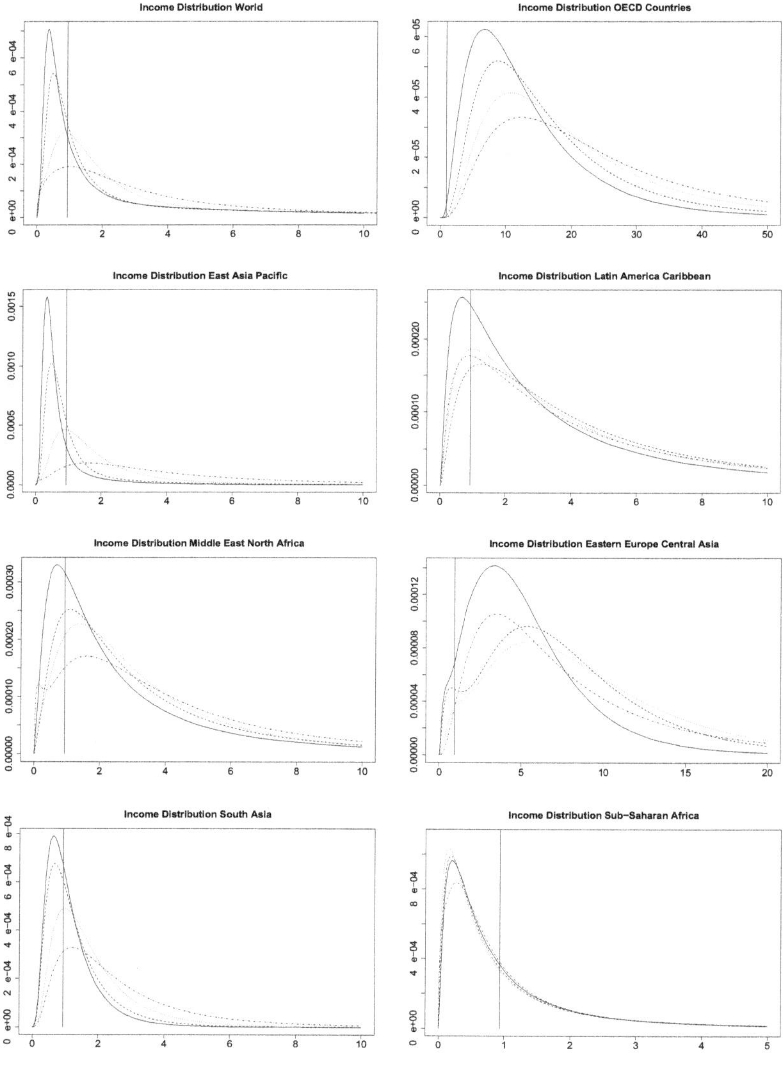

Figure C.1: Global and regional distribution of income. Solid line: 1970, dashed line: 1980, dotted line 1990, dashed-dotted: 2003.

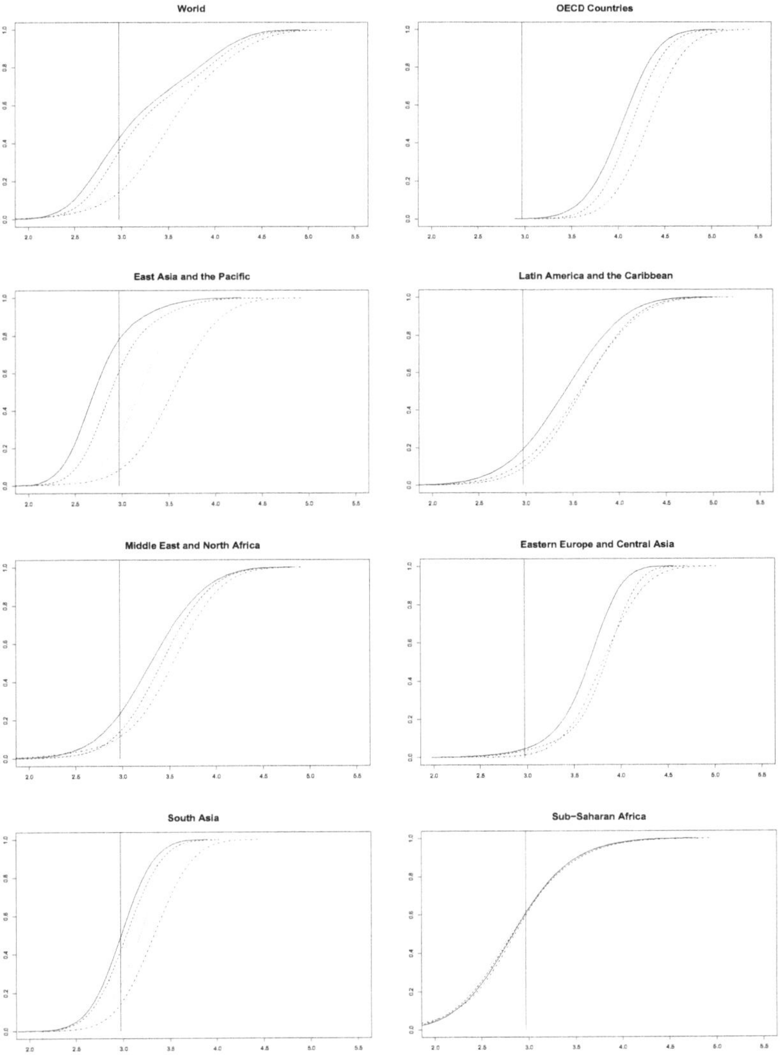

Figure C.2: Global and regional cumulative distribution of log-income. Solid line: 1970, dashed line: 1980, dotted line 1990, dashed-dotted: 2003.

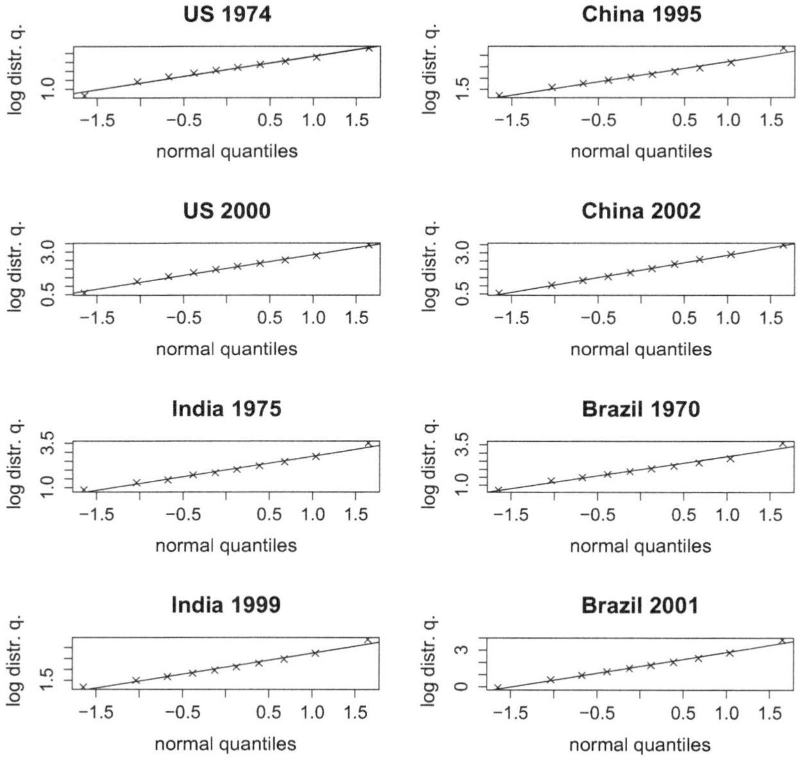

Figure C.3: Plots of log-deciles of the income distributions of the USA, China, India and Brazil for distinct years

Table C.2: Global and regional $1 and $2 per day poverty rates and poverty gap measures

Year	Poverty Rate ($1)	Poverty Rate ($2)	Poverty Gap ($1)	Poverty Gap ($2)	Poverty Rate ($1)	Poverty Rate ($2)	Poverty Gap ($1)	Poverty Gap ($2)
	World				OECD Countries			
1970	0.212	0.425	0.073	0.202	0.000	0.001	0.000	0.000
1975	0.192	0.415	0.062	0.190	0.000	0.000	0.000	0.000
1980	0.137	0.355	0.045	0.149	0.000	0.000	0.000	0.000
1985	0.083	0.272	0.029	0.102	0.000	0.000	0.000	0.000
1990	0.071	0.209	0.028	0.082	0.000	0.000	0.000	0.000
1995	0.068	0.178	0.028	0.074	0.000	0.000	0.000	0.000
2000	0.059	0.148	0.025	0.064	0.000	0.000	0.000	0.000
2003	0.058	0.142	0.025	0.062	0.000	0.000	0.000	0.000
	East Asia Pacific				Latin America Caribbean			
1970	0.454	0.782	0.153	0.403	0.073	0.191	0.026	0.079
1975	0.346	0.724	0.102	0.335	0.067	0.170	0.025	0.071
1980	0.235	0.612	0.067	0.255	0.026	0.092	0.008	0.033
1985	0.082	0.392	0.022	0.126	0.032	0.104	0.010	0.038
1990	0.057	0.250	0.017	0.082	0.040	0.121	0.013	0.046
1995	0.030	0.129	0.011	0.042	0.045	0.132	0.015	0.051
2000	0.020	0.075	0.008	0.026	0.044	0.126	0.015	0.049
2003	0.024	0.082	0.009	0.029	0.043	0.123	0.015	0.049
	Middle East North Africa				Eastern Europe and Central Asia			
1970	0.085	0.235	0.030	0.094	0.016	0.044	0.006	0.017
1975	0.069	0.205	0.024	0.080	0.010	0.032	0.003	0.012
1980	0.039	0.141	0.012	0.049	0.012	0.035	0.004	0.014
1985	0.040	0.132	0.015	0.049	0.008	0.027	0.002	0.009
1990	0.035	0.116	0.013	0.043	0.003	0.017	0.001	0.005
1995	0.047	0.113	0.021	0.050	0.006	0.033	0.001	0.009
2000	0.032	0.097	0.012	0.038	0.002	0.016	0.000	0.004
2003	0.051	0.113	0.024	0.052	0.001	0.012	0.000	0.003
	South Asia				Sub-Saharan Africa			
1970	0.138	0.487	0.036	0.175	0.367	0.609	0.169	0.335
1975	0.199	0.518	0.063	0.214	0.352	0.590	0.161	0.321
1980	0.115	0.417	0.030	0.147	0.377	0.610	0.178	0.342
1985	0.074	0.333	0.018	0.108	0.391	0.626	0.186	0.354
1990	0.042	0.236	0.009	0.070	0.396	0.620	0.196	0.359
1995	0.049	0.231	0.012	0.073	0.401	0.639	0.195	0.364
2000	0.035	0.177	0.009	0.054	0.364	0.616	0.173	0.338
2003	0.026	0.141	0.006	0.041	0.347	0.598	0.162	0.323

Table C.3: Global and regional semi-decade specific growth rates, 1970-2003.

Year	Mean of Growth Rates	Growth Rate of Mean	Rate of PPG ($1)	Rate of PPG ($2)	Mean of Growth Rates	Growth Rate of Mean	Rate of PPG ($1)	Rate of PPG ($2)
	World				OECD Countries			
1970-2003	2.332	1.830	2.192	2.679	2.000	2.079	2.210	2.210
1970-1974	1.640	2.008	2.272	1.646	2.836	2.434	4.994	4.994
1975-1979	2.421	2.195	2.280	2.789	2.636	2.729	3.493	3.493
1980-1984	2.347	0.838	4.560	4.684	1.230	1.273	2.061	2.061
1985-1989	1.850	1.867	-0.881	0.965	2.356	2.439	1.719	1.719
1990-1994	1.169	0.739	-0.005	0.817	0.750	0.936	-0.894	-0.894
1995-1999	2.397	2.009	1.285	1.697	2.061	2.106	2.580	2.580
2000-2003	1.561	1.318	0.536	0.556	0.461	0.553	-0.096	-0.096
	East Asia Pacific				Latin America Caribbean			
1970-2003	5.475	5.646	4.919	5.376	1.048	1.123	0.876	0.946
1970-1974	3.135	3.549	3.421	3.001	2.170	3.152	-0.382	0.576
1975-1979	3.607	4.630	2.165	3.084	4.198	2.217	8.298	7.212
1980-1984	6.562	4.578	9.257	8.151	-1.538	-1.557	-2.026	-1.764
1985-1989	4.024	5.299	-0.693	1.606	-0.892	0.630	-3.741	-3.131
1990-1994	6.122	6.193	4.083	5.157	0.251	1.359	-1.700	-1.501
1995-1999	4.342	4.048	2.059	3.247	0.840	1.132	0.099	0.262
2000-2003	2.520	4.068	-0.049	-1.363	0.015	-0.414	0.071	0.261
	Middle East North Africa				Eastern Europe and Central Asia			
1970-2003	1.384	1.222	0.375	1.175	1.274	1.536	2.905	2.230
1970-1974	2.771	3.127	2.196	2.230	4.240	4.144	4.563	3.946
1975-1979	3.177	1.591	6.417	5.490	2.618	2.737	-0.440	-0.321
1980-1984	0.299	0.136	-1.538	-0.121	1.793	2.003	3.065	2.635
1985-1989	-0.053	-0.676	1.592	1.094	1.431	1.586	5.790	4.881
1990-1994	1.397	1.669	-4.718	-1.196	-7.764	-5.340	-2.685	-4.197
1995-1999	2.177	2.475	8.851	5.049	1.399	0.584	7.102	5.930
2000-2003	-0.591	0.379	-13.745	-8.323	4.150	4.401	0.762	1.976
	South Asia				Sub-Saharan Africa			
1970-2003	2.397	2.654	1.856	2.106	0.045	0.264	-0.051	0.023
1970-1974	-0.316	-0.277	-0.221	-0.329	1.374	1.292	1.127	1.202
1975-1979	2.873	1.706	5.304	4.137	-0.820	0.020	-1.307	-1.160
1980-1984	2.429	2.300	3.054	2.675	-0.588	-0.385	-0.263	-0.445
1985-1989	3.048	2.914	3.065	3.207	-0.567	0.248	-1.566	-1.039
1990-1994	0.281	0.958	-1.808	-1.031	-0.610	-1.463	0.409	0.164
1995-1999	3.058	3.594	1.721	2.198	1.295	1.136	1.552	1.488
2000-2003	2.884	2.887	2.654	2.854	1.367	0.964	1.665	1.502

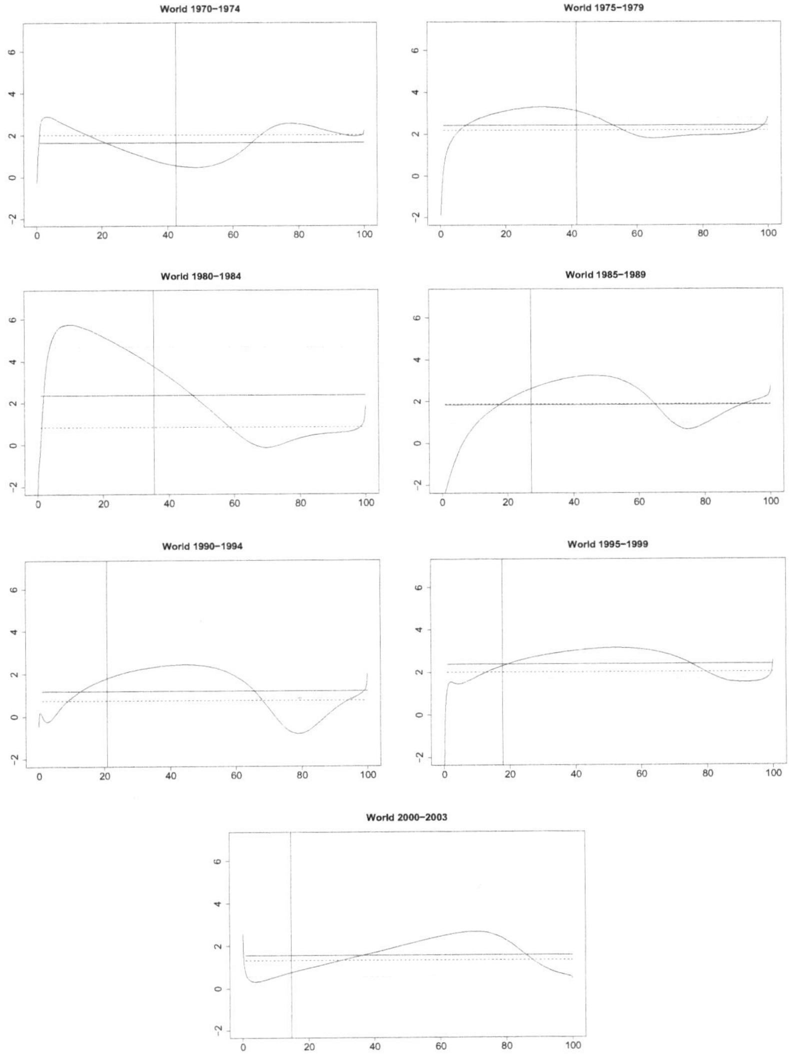

Figure C.4: Global semi-decade specific Growth Incidence Curves. Solid line: Growth Incident Curve, solid vertical line: $2 per day poverty line, solid horizontal line: mean of growth rates, dashed line: growth rate of mean, dotted line: rate of pro-poor growth.

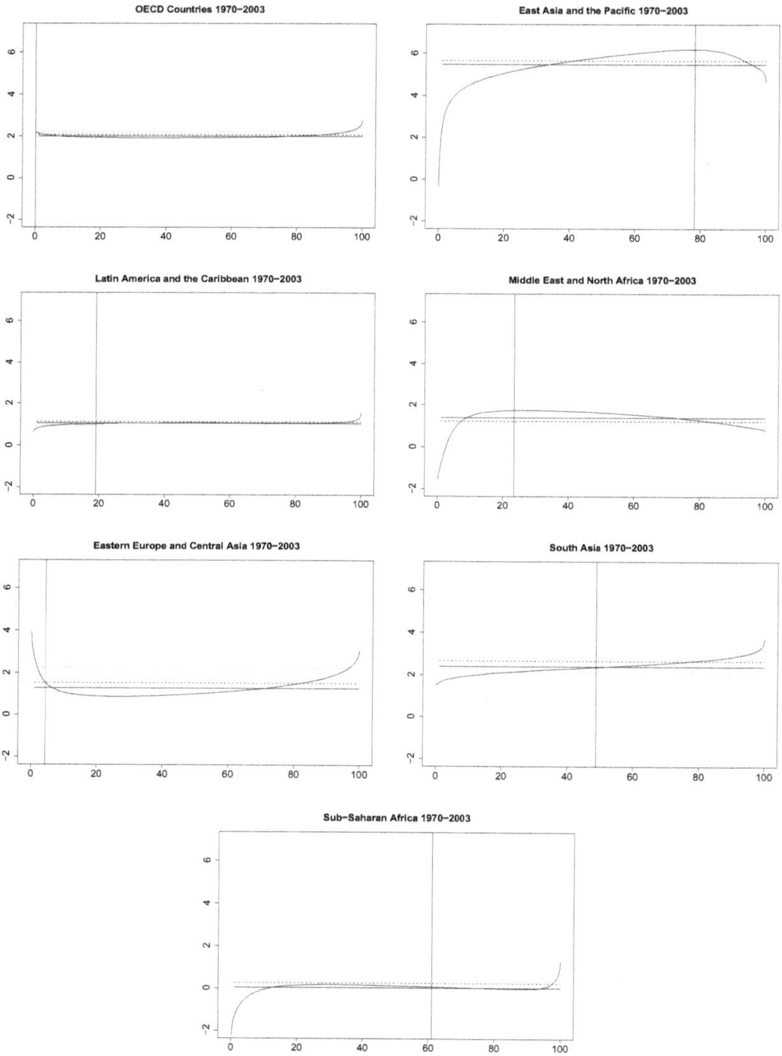

Figure C.5: Regional Growth Incidence Curves, 1970-2003. Solid line: Growth Incident Curve, solid vertical line: $2 per day poverty line, solid horizontal line: mean of growth rates, dashed line: growth rate of mean, dotted line: rate of pro-poor growth.

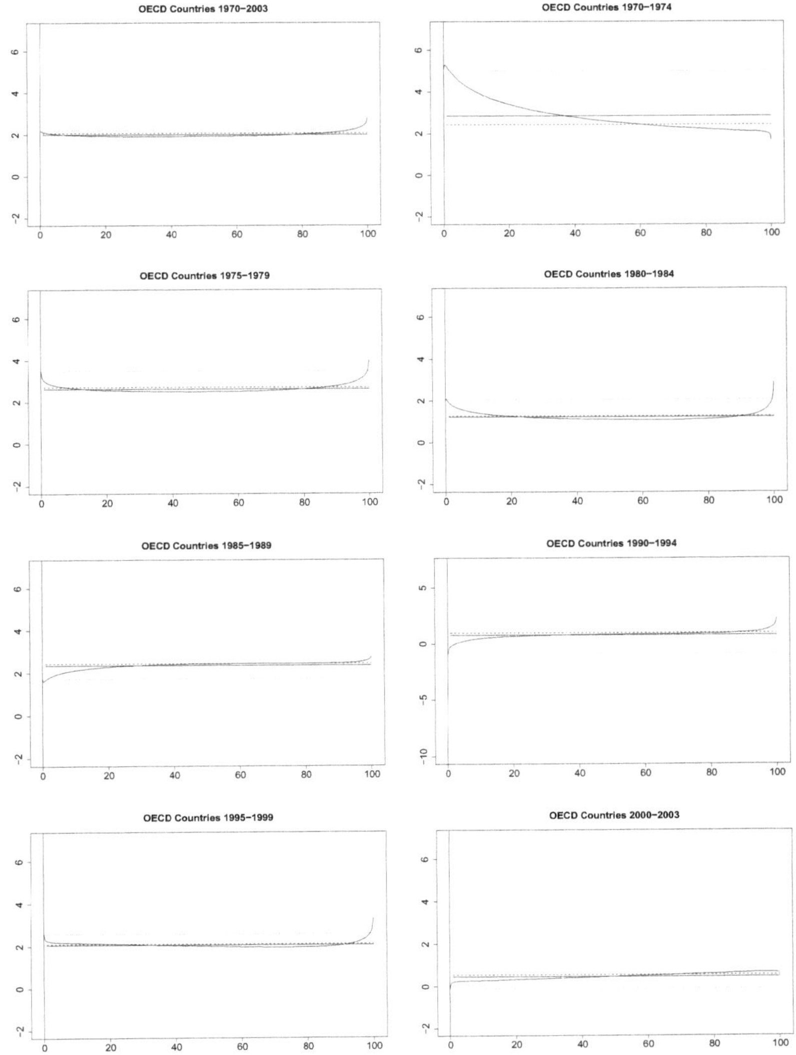

Figure C.6: Semi-decade specific Growth Incidence Curves, OECD countries. Solid line: Growth Incident Curve, solid vertical line: \$2 per day poverty line, solid horizontal line: mean of growth rates, dashed line: growth rate of mean, dotted line: rate of pro-poor growth.

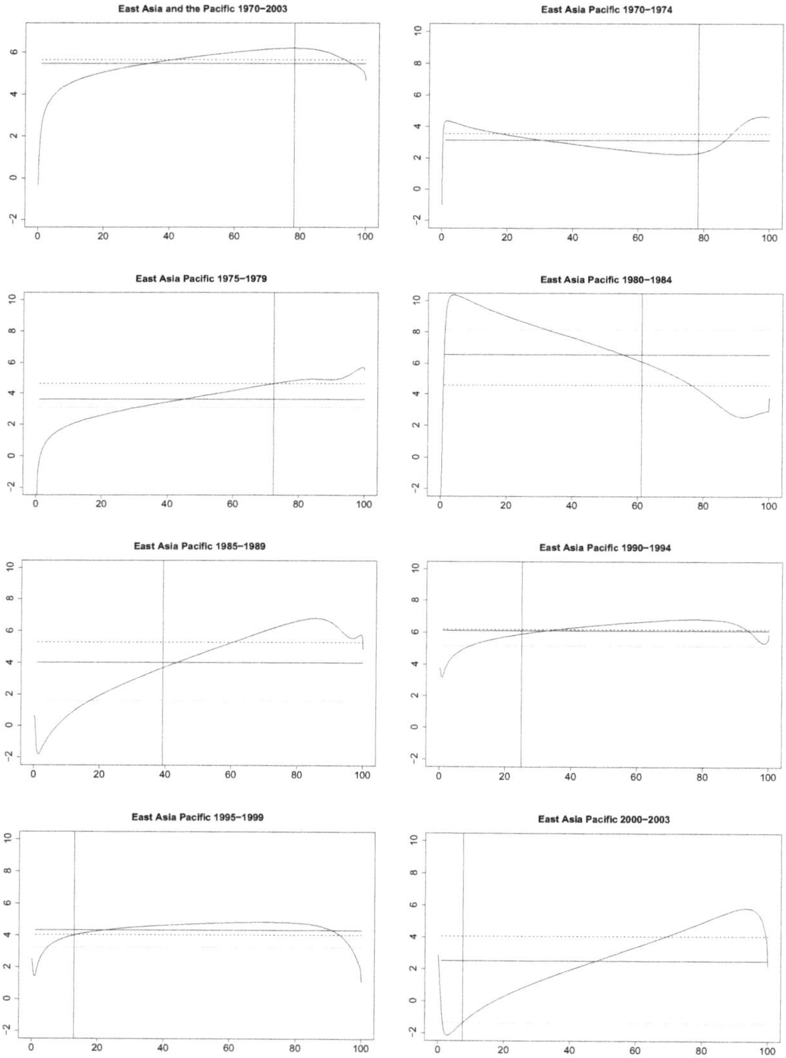

Figure C.7: Semi-decade specific Growth Incidence Curves, East Asia and the Pacific. Solid line: Growth Incident Curve, solid vertical line: $2 per day poverty line, solid horizontal line: mean of growth rates, dashed line: growth rate of mean, dotted line: rate of pro-poor growth.

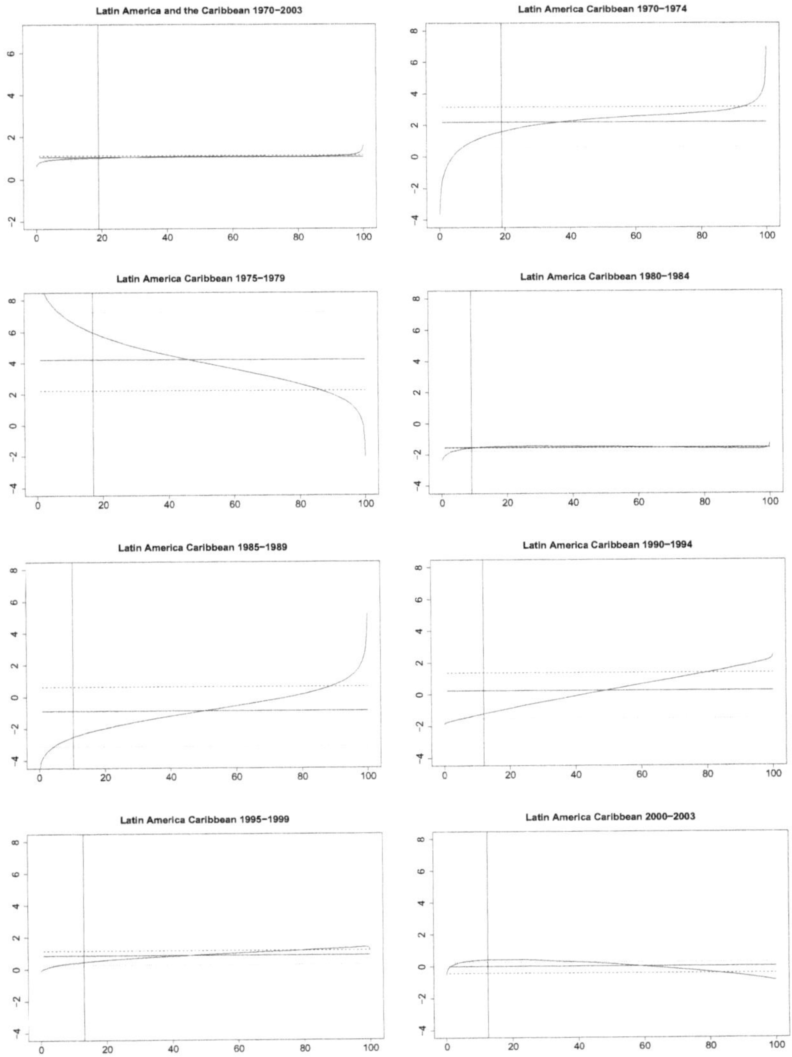

Figure C.8: Semi-decade specific Growth Incidence Curves, Latin America and the Caribbean. Solid line: Growth Incident Curve, solid vertical line: $2 per day poverty line, solid horizontal line: mean of growth rates, dashed line: growth rate of mean, dotted line: rate of pro-poor growth.

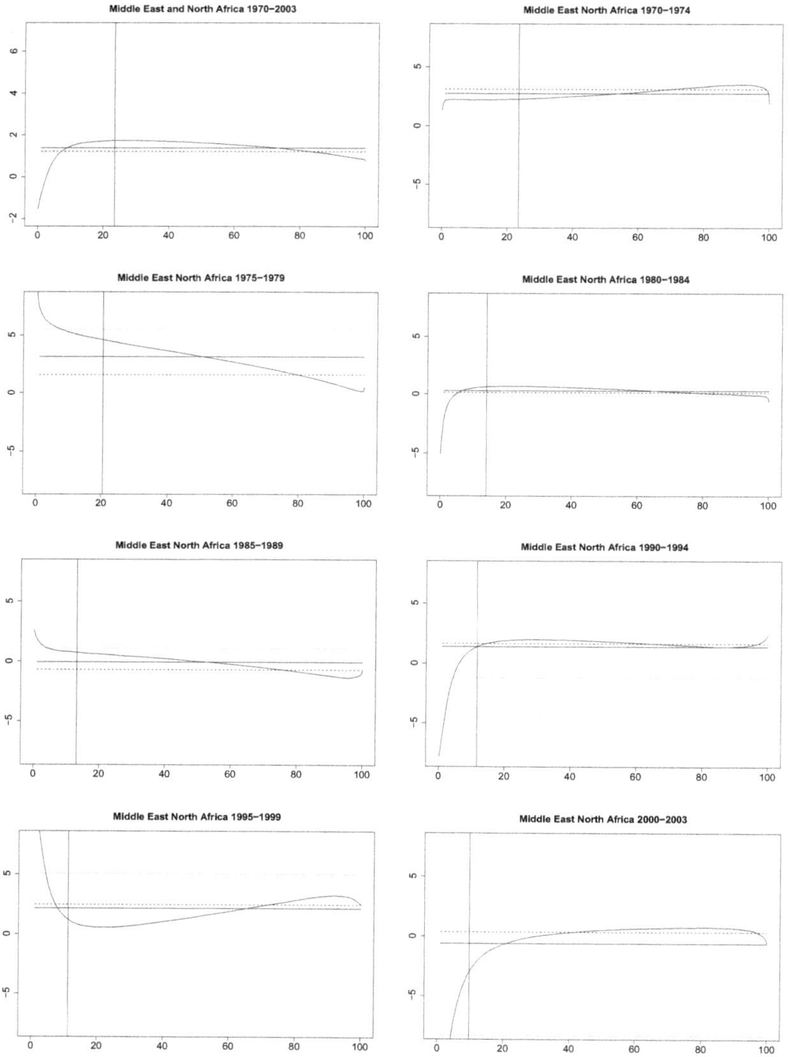

Figure C.9: Semi-decade specific Growth Incidence Curves, Middle East and North Africa. Solid line: Growth Incident Curve, solid vertical line: \$2 per day poverty line, solid horizontal line: mean of growth rates, dashed line: growth rate of mean, dotted line: rate of pro-poor growth.

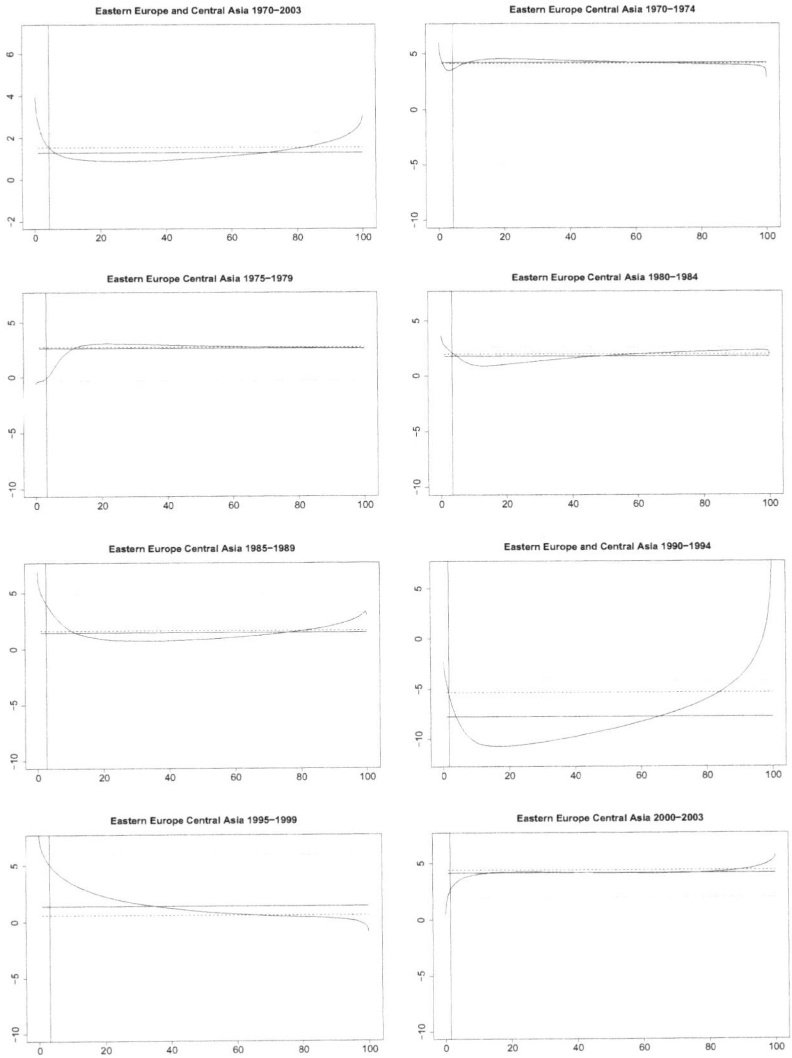

Figure C.10: Semi-decade specific Growth Incidence Curves, Eastern Europe and Central Asia. Solid line: Growth Incident Curve, solid vertical line: $2 per day poverty line, solid horizontal line: mean of growth rates, dashed line: growth rate of mean, dotted line: rate of pro-poor growth.

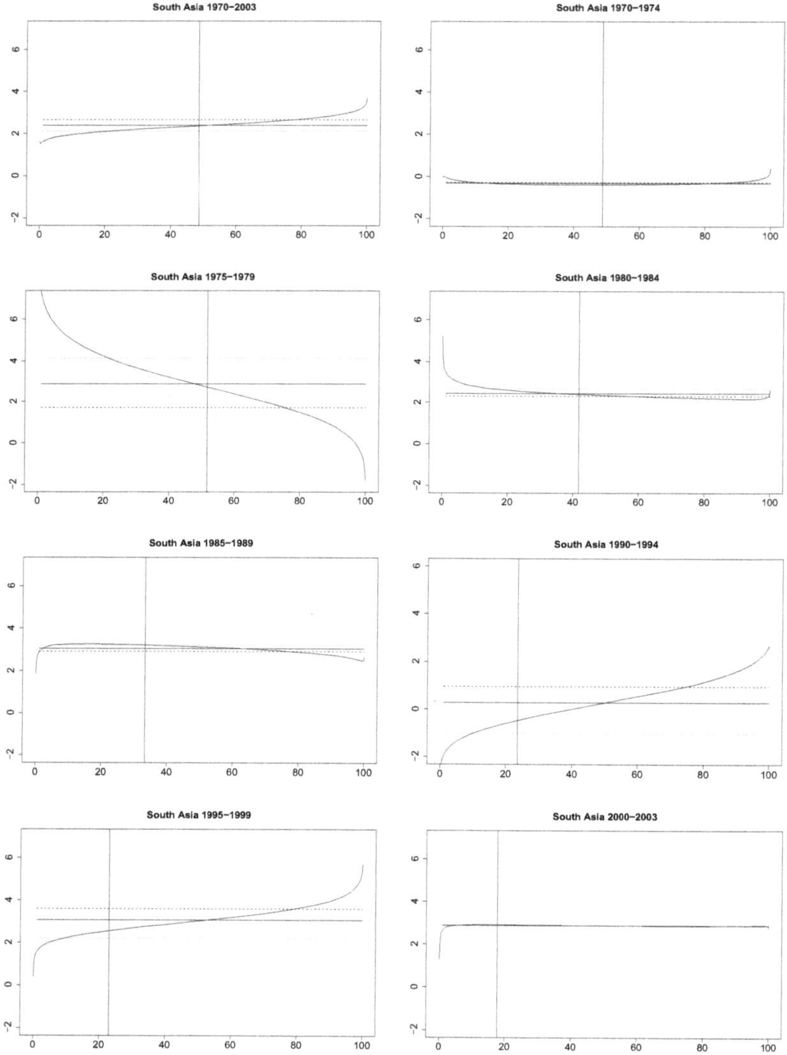

Figure C.11: Semi-decade specific Growth Incidence Curves, South Asia. Solid line: Growth Incident Curve, solid vertical line: $2 per day poverty line, solid horizontal line: mean of growth rates, dashed line: growth rate of mean, dotted line: rate of pro-poor growth.

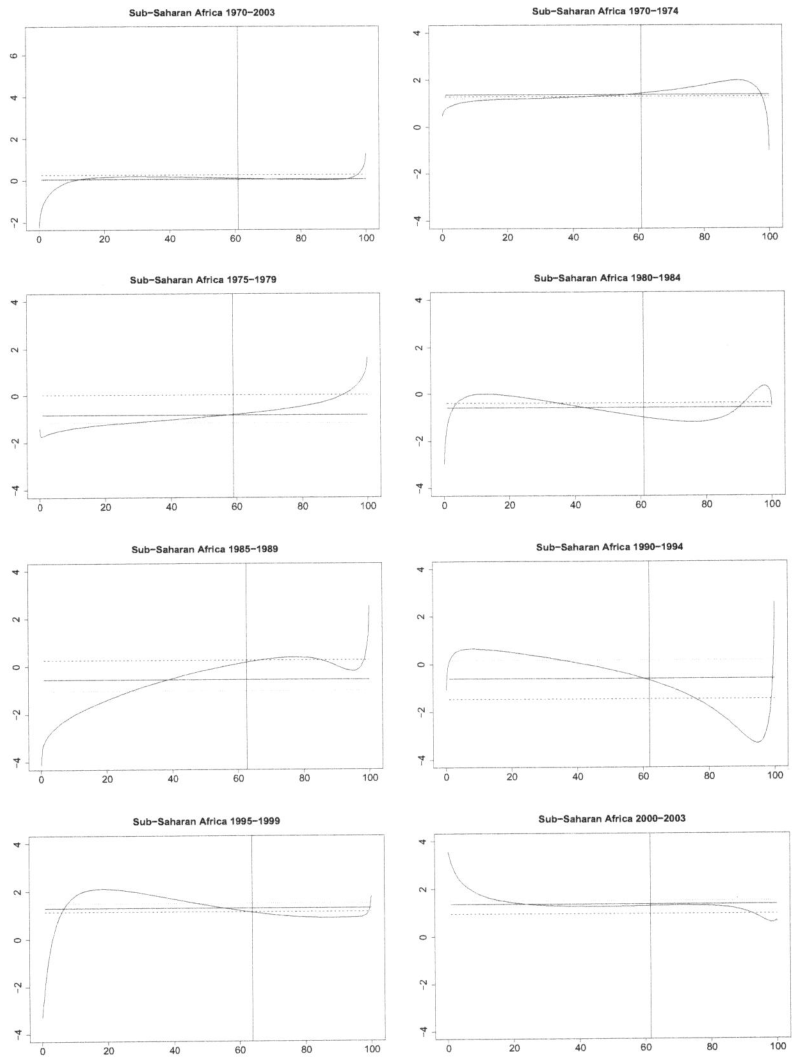

Figure C.12: Semi-decade specific Growth Incidence Curves, Sub-Saharan Africa. Solid line: Growth Incident Curve, solid vertical line: \$2 per day poverty line, solid horizontal line: mean of growth rates, dashed line: growth rate of mean, dotted line: rate of pro-poor growth.

Appendix to Essay 4

Table D.1: Import demand elasticity for each 1 digit HS category, EU 25

	HS0	HS1	HS2	HS3	HS4	HS5	HS6	HS7	HS8	HS9
Uganda	-0.857***	-0.946*	-1.113***	-1.162***	-1.113***	-0.603*	-1.024***	-1.016***	-0.855***	-0.945***
	(0.242)	(0.442)	(0.122)	(0.133)	(0.201)	(0.257)	(0.074)	(0.136)	(0.056)	(0.088)
Tanzania	-0.830***	-1.337***	-1.256***	-1.081***	-0.486*	-0.526**	-0.223*	-0.544***	-0.975***	-0.694***
	(0.173)	(0.305)	(0.108)	(0.106)	(0.218)	(0.160)	(0.094)	(0.131)	(0.085)	(0.108)
Mozambique	-1.198***	-0.487*	-1.316***	-1.044***	-0.930***	-0.526***	-1.061***	-1.010***	-0.785***	-0.762***
	(0.132)	(0.234)	(0.158)	(0.167)	(0.144)	(0.105)	(0.086)	(0.071)	(0.044)	(0.074)
Ghana	-0.626*	-1.408***	-0.905***	-1.146***	-1.320***	-0.586***	-0.416***	-1.048***	-0.933***	-0.368
	(0.309)	(0.339)	(0.202)	(0.204)	(0.144)	(0.107)	(0.103)	(0.126)	(0.120)	(0.234)
Côte d'Ivoire	-1.680***	-2.320***	-1.904***	-2.386***	-1.573***	-1.115***	-1.173***	-1.466***	-1.104***	-1.052***
	(0.271)	(0.387)	(0.314)	(0.230)	(0.319)	(0.221)	(0.134)	(0.183)	(0.092)	(0.201)
Botswana	-0.726**	-1.027***	-1.890***	-1.042***	-1.217***	-0.575*	-0.667***	-0.762***	-0.971***	-0.713***
	(0.276)	(0.207)	(0.251)	(0.186)	(0.177)	(0.244)	(0.176)	(0.209)	(0.083)	(0.148)
Kenya	-1.115***	-1.103***	-1.415***	-0.854***	-1.186***	-0.898***	-0.877***	-0.937***	-0.954***	-0.892***
	(0.178)	(0.133)	(0.169)	(0.159)	(0.125)	(0.136)	(0.106)	(0.082)	(0.061)	(0.142)
Namibia	-0.880***	-0.905**	-1.172***	-0.987***	-0.992***	-0.731***	-0.700***	-0.475**	-0.737***	-0.609***
	(0.168)	(0.275)	(0.178)	(0.143)	(0.129)	(0.188)	(0.123)	(0.158)	(0.084)	(0.123)
Cameroon	-1.951***	-2.787***	-1.941***	-1.683***	-1.528***	-1.240***	-0.729***	-1.846***	-1.275***	-1.019***
	(0.300)	(0.426)	(0.319)	(0.156)	(0.153)	(0.163)	(0.168)	(0.243)	(0.115)	(0.245)
Fixed Effects					YES					
R-squared	0.726	0.652	0.726	0.773	0.780	0.693	0.842	0.774	0.793	0.737
AIC	4009.242	3724.583	7775.706	6681.943	5548.05	3588.515	6046.93	6134.704	14866.76	5626.691
BIC	4096.959	3809.87	7876.277	6780.732	5642.407	3673.106	6142.423	6230.793	14981.22	5722.245
N	966	844	1973	1787	1397	812	1488	1538	4266	1493

Note: *** denotes significance at 1 percent level, ** denotes significance at 5 percent level. Standard errors are reported in brackets.

Table D.2: Import demand elasticity for each 1 digit HS category, Sub-Saharan Africa

	HS0	HS1	HS2	HS3	HS4	HS5	HS6	HS7	HS8	HS9
Uganda	-0.686*	-0.297	-0.568***	-0.983**	-0.571***	-0.748**	-0.964***	-0.665***	-0.611***	-0.578***
	(0.311)	(0.439)	(0.159)	(0.353)	(0.173)	(0.243)	(0.134)	(0.163)	(0.061)	(0.174)
Tanzania	-0.902**	-1.071***	-0.892***	-0.507***	-0.738***	-0.729***	-0.738***	-1.038***	-0.885***	-0.760***
	(0.301)	(0.291)	(0.125)	(0.151)	(0.146)	(0.185)	(0.167)	(0.199)	(0.072)	(0.127)
Mozambique	-1.234***	-1.126***	-1.222***	-1.060***	-1.319***	-1.072***	-1.227***	-1.022***	-0.827***	-0.965***
	(0.229)	(0.272)	(0.113)	(0.140)	(0.142)	(0.113)	(0.067)	(0.079)	(0.074)	(0.071)
Ghana	-0.871***	-0.103	-0.722***	-0.633***	-0.742***	-0.137	-1.000***	-0.548***	-0.609***	-0.478***
	(0.263)	(0.244)	(0.154)	(0.137)	(0.172)	(0.189)	(0.139)	(0.141)	(0.125)	(0.098)
Côte d'Ivoire	-0.971***	-1.618**	-0.960*	-0.765***	-0.753***	-1.304**	-1.143***	-1.083***	-0.532***	-0.740***
	(0.212)	(0.530)	(0.431)	(0.212)	(0.226)	(0.436)	(0.249)	(0.326)	(0.127)	(0.205)
Botswana	1.595***	-0.618	0.330	-0.151	-1.122***	-1.500***	-1.243***	-0.745*	0.025	-0.068
	(0.355)	(0.465)	(0.766)	(0.241)	(0.336)	(0.302)	(0.060)	(0.304)	(0.174)	(0.258)
Kenya	-0.942**	-1.621***	-1.028***	-0.997***	-1.230***	-0.650**	-0.758***	-1.120***	-0.979***	-0.911***
	(0.297)	(0.306)	(0.112)	(0.096)	(0.125)	(0.243)	(0.115)	(0.096)	(0.067)	(0.131)
Namibia	-0.437	-2.886**	-0.807*	-4.073***	-0.491	-1.175***	-1.354***	-0.245	-0.255*	-0.530
	(0.630)	(0.986)	(0.397)	(0.620)	(0.333)	(0.265)	(0.206)	(0.373)	(0.120)	(0.283)
Cameroon	-0.300	-2.559**	-0.536	-0.960***	-0.642	-0.055	-0.530	-0.188	-0.731***	-0.296
	(0.620)	(0.837)	(0.664)	(0.254)	(0.422)	(0.382)	(0.327)	(0.212)	(0.113)	(0.180)
Fixed Effects					YES					
R-squared	0.556	0.560	0.591	0.716	0.716	0.663	0.797	0.706	0.815	0.775
AIC	3837.857	3884.921	7641.013	6734.74	5167.006	4270.725	4998.589	5952.82	13235.19	4965.852
BIC	3927.263	3972.051	7742.168	6833.377	5261.182	4359.875	5092.661	6049.507	13347.58	5059.527
N	1061	935	2038	1772	1383	1046	1375	1590	3804	1345

Note: *** denotes significance at 1 percent level, ** denotes significance at 5 percent level. Standard errors are reported in brackets.

Table D.3: Short-run welfare effects of a tariff reduction according to the interim agreements (after five years)

	Botswana	Côte d'Ivoire	Cameroon	Ghana	Kenya	Mozambique	Namibia	Tanzania	Uganda
All products									
Consumption	60.68	1459.97	54	86.64	689.34	12.26	14.87	27.35	29.23
Diversion	-275.91	-6870.85	-271.2	-3912.16	-26641.35	-1365.95	-957.47	-20998.8	-3702.75
Creation	163104.9	7456.67	390.88	300.23	5520.45	33701.15	246969.7	4754.79	3883.86
Total	162889.7	2045.79	173.68	-3525.29	-20431.56	32347.46	246027.1	-16216.65	210.34
in %	5.35%	0.03%	0.01%	-0.04%	-0.36%	2.02%	10.07%	-0.55%	0.01%
Revenue	-1905.1	-42732.96	-3064.91	-11960.81	-78259.52	-4868.95	-2354.41	-44151.47	-8585.84
Non-manufacturing									
Consumption	60.67	762.46	15.23	27.08	1	3.55	0.66	13.2	0
Diversion	-11.96	-1373.6	-21.75	-1649.25	-73.26	-118.86	-7.59	-106.34	-118.94
Creation	8194.93	6686.75	293.25	258.81	675.66	4993.73	56452.78	16.14	619.1
Total	8243.64	6075.61	286.73	-1363.36	603.41	4878.42	56445.84	-76.99	500.16
in %	0.69%	0.18%	0.02%	-0.05%	0.03%	0.88%	7.89%	-0.01%	0.08%
Revenue	-1329.63	-14588.26	-713.72	-4290.16	-169.6	-409.44	-86.97	-400.74	-242.44
Manufacturing									
Consumption	0	697.51	38.77	59.56	688.34	8.71	14.22	14.15	29.23
Diversion	-265.21	-5497.24	-249.46	-2262.92	-26568.09	-1247.1	-949.89	-20892.46	-3583.81
Creation	150199.3	769.91	97.63	41.42	4844.78	28707.43	190464	4738.65	3264.76
Total	149934	-4029.82	-113.05	-2161.94	-21034.97	27469.04	189528.4	-16139.66	-289.82
in %	8.12%	-0.13%	-0.01%	-0.04%	-0.53%	2.63%	10.97%	-0.72%	-0.02%
Revenue	-575.47	-28144.7	-2351.19	-7670.65	-78089.91	-4459.51	-2267.44	-43750.73	-8343.4

Note: Units are 1000 USD.

Appendix to Essay 5

Table E.1: Countries classified by political system, GDP per capita and life expectancy, 1970

	Low life expectancy Mean: 44.28; Min: 34.75; Max: 51.83; Obs: 48		**Middle life expectancy** Mean: 58.87; Min: 51.85; Max: 66.16; Obs 48		**High life expectancy** Mean: 70.33; Min: 66.28; Max: 74.43; Obs: 47	
	Autocracies	**Democracies**	**Autocracies**	**Democracies**	**Autocracies**	**Democracies**
Low income	Benin; Bhutan; Burkina Faso; Burundi; Cambodia; Central African Republic; Chad; Congo, Dem. Rep.; Equatorial Guinea; Ethiopia; Indonesia; Lao PDR; Lesotho; Madagascar; Malawi; Mali; Mauritania; Nepal; Niger; Nigeria; Pakistan; Rwanda; Senegal; Somalia; Sudan; Tanzania; Togo; Uganda; Zambia	The Gambia; Ghana; India; Sierra Leone	China; Congo, Rep.; Kenya; Korea, Dem. Rep.; Mongolia; Syrian Arab Republic	Botswana; Sri Lanka	-	Comoros; Guinea-Bissau; Maldives; Mozambique
Middle income	Afghanistan; Bolivia; Cameroon; Egypt. Arab Rep.; Guinea; Haiti; Liberia; Morocco; Swaziland	-	Algeria; Brazil; Dominican Republic; Ecuador; El Salvador; Honduras; Iraq; Jordan; Mexico; Panama; Paraguay; Peru; Tunisia	Colombia; Fiji; Guatemala; Korea, Rep.; Malaysia; Mauritius; Philippines; Thailand; Turkey; Zimbabwe	Cuba; Poland; Romania	Jamaica
High income	Gabon; Oman; Saudi Arabia	-	Iran, Islamic Rep.; Kuwait; Nicaragua	Chile; South Africa; Trinidad and Tobago; Venezuela, RB	Argentina; Greece; Hungary; Portugal; Singapore; Spain	Australia; Austria; Belgium; Canada; Costa Rica; Cyprus; Denmark; Finland; France; Ireland; Israel; Italy; Japan; Netherlands; New Zealand; Norway; Sweden; Switzerland; United Kingdom; United States; Uruguay

Table E.2: Countries classified by political system, GDP per capita and life expectancy, 1980

	Low life expectancy Mean: 47.88; Min: 37.59; Max: 56.29		Middle life expectancy Mean: 62.63; Min: 56.43; Max: 68.60		High life expectancy Mean: 71.96; Min: 68.94; Max: 76.25	
	Autocracies	**Democracies**	**Autocracies**	**Democracies**	**Autocracies**	**Democracies**
Low income	Afghanistan; Bangladesh; Benin; Bhutan; Burkina Faso; Burundi; Central African Republic; Chad; Comoros; Congo, Dem. Rep.; Congo, Rep.; Equatorial Guinea; Ethiopia; Guinea-Bissau; Indonesia; Lao PDR; Lesotho; Liberia; Madagascar; Malawi; Mali; Mauritania; Mozambique; Nepal; Niger; Pakistan; Rwanda; Senegal; Sierra Leone; Somalia; Sudan; Tanzania; Togo; Zambia	The Gambia; Ghana; India; Maldives; Nigeria; Uganda	China; Kenya; Korea, Dem. Rep.; Mongolia; Syrian Arab Republic	Sri Lanka	-	-
Middle income	Bolivia; Cameroon; Djibouti; Egypt. Arab Rep.; El Salvador; Guinea; Haiti; Swaziland	Papua New Guinea	Algeria; Brazil; Guatemala; Iran, Islamic Rep.; Iraq; Jordan; Korea, Rep.; Mexico; Morocco; Nicaragua; Paraguay; Philippines; Tunisia; Turkey	Botswana; Colombia; Dominican Republic; Ecuador; Fiji; Honduras; Malaysia; Mauritius; Peru; Solomon Islands; South Africa; Thailand; Zimbabwe	Chile; Cuba; Panama; Poland; Romania	Costa Rica; Jamaica
High income	Gabon	-	Bahrain; Oman; Qatar; Saudi Arabia; United Arab Emirates	Venezuela, RB	Argentina; Hungary; Kuwait; Singapore; Uruguay	Australia; Austria; Belgium; Brunei; Canada; Cyprus; Denmark; Finland; France; Greece; Ireland; Israel; Italy; Japan; Netherlands; New Zealand; Norway; Portugal; Spain; Sweden; Switzerland; Trinidad and Tobago; United Kingdom; United States

Table E.3: Countries classified by political system, GDP per capita and life expectancy, 1990

	Low life expectancy Mean: 48.71; Min: 37.54; Max: 61.31 **Autocracies**	**Democracies**	Middle life expectancy Mean: 67.62; Min: 61.36; Max: 72.18 **Autocracies**	**Democracies**	High life expectancy Mean: 76.24; Min: 72.45; Max: 81.23 **Autocracies**	**Democracies**
Low income	Afghanistan; Angola; Bhutan; Burkina Faso; Burundi; Chad; Congo, Dem. Rep.; Congo, Rep. Eritrea; The Gambia; Haiti; Kenya; Lao PDR; Liberia; Mauritania; Rwanda; Sierra Leone; Somalia; Sudan; Togo; Uganda; Yemen. Rep.	Benin; Cambodia; Central African Republic; Cote d'Ivoire; Ethiopia; Ghana; Guinea-Bissau; Lesotho; Madagascar; Malawi; Mali; Mozambique; Nepal; Niger; Nigeria; Senegal; Tanzania; Zambia	Korea, Dem. Rep.; Solomon Islands; Tajikistan; Vietnam	Bangladesh; Honduras; Moldova; Mongolia	Syrian Arab Republic	Serbia and Montenegro
Middle income	Cameroon; Equatorial Guinea; Guinea; Iraq; Pakistan; Swaziland; Zimbabwe	Botswana; Djibouti; Guyana; Namibia; Papua New Guinea; South Africa	Algeria; Azerbaijan; Belarus; China; Egypt. Arab Rep.; Jordan; Kazakhstan; Kyrgyz Republic; Morocco; Pakistan; Turkmenistan; Uzbekistan	Armenia; Bolivia; Brazil; Bulgaria; Colombia; Dominican Republic; El Salvador; Fiji; Georgia; Guatemala; Guyana; India; Indonesia; Iran, Islamic Rep.; Jamaica; Latvia; Lithuania; Nicaragua; Paraguay; Philippines; Romania; Russian Federation; Thailand Turkey; Ukraine	Cuba; Libya; Tunisia	Albania; Costa Rica; Croatia; Ecuador; Macedonia, FYR; Mexico; Panama; Poland; Slovak Republic; Sri Lanka; Venezuela, RB
High income	Gabon	-	Qatar; Saudi Arabia	Estonia; Hungary; Mauritius; Trinidad and Tobago	Bahrain; Kuwait; Oman; Singapore; United Arab Emirates	Argentina; Australia; Austria; Belgium; Canada; Chile; Cyprus; Czech Republic; Denmark; Finland; France; Germany; Greece; Ireland; Israel; Italy; Japan; Korea, Rep.; Malaysia; Netherlands; New Zealand; Norway; Portugal; Slovenia; Spain; Sweden; Switzerland; United Kingdom; United States; Uruguay

Table E.4: Countries classified by political system, GDP per capita and life expectancy, 2000

	Low life expectancy Mean: 48.71; Min: 37.54; Max: 61.31		Middle life expectancy Mean: 67.62; Min: 61.36; Max: 72.18		High life expectancy Mean: 76.24; Min: 72.45; Max: 81.23	
	Autocracies	**Democracies**	**Autocracies**	**Democracies**	**Autocracies**	**Democracies**
Low income	Afghanistan; Angola; Bhutan; Burkina Faso; Burundi; Chad; Congo, Dem. Rep.; Congo, Rep. Eritrea; The Gambia; Haiti; Kenya; Lao PDR; Liberia; Mauritania; Rwanda; Sierra Leone; Somalia; Sudan; Togo; Uganda; Yemen. Rep.	Benin; Cambodia; Central African Republic; Cote d'Ivoire; Ethiopia; Ghana; Guinea-Bissau; Lesotho; Madagascar; Malawi; Mali; Mozambique; Nepal; Niger; Nigeria; Senegal; Tanzania; Zambia	Korea, Dem. Rep.; Solomon Islands; Tajikistan; Vietnam	Bangladesh; Honduras; Moldova; Mongolia	Syrian Arab Republic	Serbia and Montenegro
Middle income	Cameroon; Equatorial Guinea; Guinea; Iraq; Pakistan; Swaziland; Zimbabwe	Botswana; Djibouti; Guyana; Namibia; Papua New Guinea; South Africa	Algeria; Azerbaijan; Belarus; China; Egypt. Arab Rep.; Jordan; Kazakhstan; Kyrgyz Republic; Morocco; Pakistan; Turkmenistan; Uzbekistan	Armenia; Bolivia; Brazil; Bulgaria; Colombia; Dominican Republic; El Salvador; Fiji; Georgia; Guatemala; Guyana; India; Indonesia; Iran, Islamic Rep.; Jamaica; Latvia; Lithuania; Nicaragua; Paraguay; Philippines; Romania; Russian Federation; Thailand Turkey; Ukraine	Cuba; Libya; Tunisia	Albania; Costa Rica; Croatia; Ecuador; Macedonia, FYR; Mexico; Panama; Poland; Slovak Republic; Sri Lanka; Venezuela, RB
High income	Gabon	-	Qatar; Saudi Arabia	Estonia; Hungary; Mauritius; Trinidad and Tobago	Bahrain; Kuwait; Oman; Singapore; United Arab Emirates	Argentina; Australia; Austria; Belgium; Canada; Chile; Cyprus; Czech Republic; Denmark; Finland; France; Germany; Greece; Ireland; Israel; Italy; Japan; Korea, Rep.; Malaysia; Netherlands; New Zealand; Norway; Portugal; Slovenia; Spain; Sweden; Switzerland; United Kingdom; United States; Uruguay

Table E.5: Countries classified by political system, GDP per capita and literacy, 1970

	Low literacy rate Mean: 21.30; Min: 5.75; Max: 35.36		Middle literacy rate Mean: 54.21; Min: 35.64; Max: 72.89		High literacy rate Mean: 89.07; Min: 73.21; Max: 99	
	Autocracies	**Democracies**	**Autocracies**	**Democracies**	**Autocracies**	**Democracies**
Low income	Benin; Burkina Faso; Burundi; Central African Republic; Chad; Congo, Dem. Rep.; Congo, Rep.; Ethiopia; Mali; Mauritania; Nepal; Niger; Nigeria; Pakistan; Rwanda; Senegal; Sudan; Togo	The Gambia; Ghana; India	Cambodia; China; Equatorial Guinea; Indonesia; Kenya; Lao PDR; Lesotho; Madagascar; Malawi; Syrian Arab Republic; Tanzania; Uganda; Zambia	Botswana	Mongolia	Sri Lanka
Middle income	Algeria; Cameroon; Egypt, Arab Rep.; Haiti; Iraq; Liberia; Morocco; Tunisia	-	Bolivia; Brazil; Dominican Republic; El Salvador; Honduras; Jordan; Peru; Swaziland	Guatemala; Jamaica; Malaysia; Mauritius; Zimbabwe	Cuba; Ecuador; Panama; Paraguay; Romania	Colombia; Fiji; Philippines; Thailand
High income	Iran, Islamic Rep.; Oman; Saudi Arabia	-	Kuwait; Nicaragua; Singapore	South Africa	Argentina	Chile; Costa Rica; Cyprus; Israel; Trinidad and Tobago; Uruguay; Venezuela, RB

Table E.6: Countries classified by political system, GDP per capita and literacy, 1980

	Low literacy rate Mean: 29.76; Min: 7.95; Max: 47.55		**Middle literacy rate** Mean: 63.11; Min: 48.18; Max: 76.27		**High literacy rate** Mean: 91.90; Min: 79.43; Max: 99	
	Autocracies	**Democracies**	**Autocracies**	**Democracies**	**Autocracies**	**Democracies**
Low income	Bangladesh; Benin; Burkina Faso; Burundi; Central African Republic; Chad; Congo, Dem. Rep.; Ethiopia; Guinea-Bissau; Liberia; Madagascar; Malawi; Mali; Mauritania; Mozambique; Nepal; Niger; Pakistan; Rwanda; Senegal; Sudan; Togo	The Gambia; Ghana; India; Nigeria; Uganda	China; Comoros; Congo, Rep.; Equatorial Guinea; Indonesia; Kenya; Lao, PDR; Lesotho; Syrian Arab Republic; Tanzania; Zambia	-	Mongolia	Sri Lanka
Middle income	Algeria; Cameroon; Djibouti; Egypt, Arab Rep.; Haiti; Iraq; Morocco; Tunisia	-	Bolivia; Brazil; El Salvador; Guatemala; Iran, Islamic Rep.; Jordan; Nicaragua; Swaziland	Botswana; Dominican Republic; Honduras; Jamaica; Malaysia; Mauritius; Papua New Guinea; South Africa; Zimbabwe	Chile; Cuba; Panama; Paraguay; Philippines; Romania	Colombia; Costa Rica; Ecuador; Fiji; Peru; Thailand
High income	Oman	-	Bahrain; Kuwait; Qatar; Saudi Arabia; United Arab Emirates	-	Argentina; Singapore; Uruguay	Cyprus; Israel; Trinidad and Tobago; Venezuela, RB

Table E.7: Countries classified by political system, GDP per capita and literacy, 1990

	Low literacy rate Mean: 39.57; Min: 11.40; Max: 57.88		Middle literacy rate Mean: 72.17; Min: 57.96; Max: 82.18		High literacy rate Mean: 94.530; Min: 85.47; Max: 99	
	Autocracies	**Democracies**	**Autocracies**	**Democracies**	**Autocracies**	**Democracies**
Low income	Bangladesh; Benin; Burkina Faso; Burundi; Central African Republic; Chad; Congo, Dem. Rep.; Ethiopia; Guinea-Bissau; Lao, PDR.; Liberia; Malawi; Mali; Mauritania; Mozambique; Niger; Nigeria; Rwanda; Senegal; Sudan; Togo; Uganda; Yemen, Rep.	Comoros; The Gambia; Haiti; India; Nepal	China; Equatorial Guinea; Ghana; Kenya; Lesotho; Madagascar; Syrian Arab Republic; Tanzania; Zambia	*Cambodia*	Vietnam	*Mongolia*
Middle income	Algeria; Cameroon; Djibouti; Egypt, Arab Rep.; Iraq; Morocco	Pakistan; Papua New Guinea	Congo, Rep.; Indonesia; Iran, Islamic Rep.; Jordan; Swaziland; Tunisia; Zimbabwe	Albania; Bolivia; Brazil; Botswana; Dominican Republic; El Salvador; Guatemala; Honduras; Jamaica; Malaysia; Namibia; Nicaragua; South Africa	Cuba; Uzbekistan	Argentina; Chile; Colombia; Costa Rica; Ecuador; Fiji; Panama; Paraguay; Peru; Philippines; Romania; Sri Lanka; Thailand; Uruguay; Venezuela, RB
High income	Oman	-	Bahrain; Qatar; Saudi Arabia; United Arab Emirates	Mauritius	Croatia; Estonia; Russian Federation; Singapore; Slovenia	Cyprus; Israel; Trinidad and Tobago

Table E.8: Countries classified by political system, GDP per capita and literacy, 2000

	Low literacy rate Mean: 49.74; Min: 15.96; Max: 67.03		Middle literacy rate Mean: 80.03; Min: 68.01; Max: 88.67		High literacy rate Mean: 96.27; Min: 89.81389; Max: 99	
	Autocracies	**Democracies**	**Autocracies**	**Democracies**	**Autocracies**	**Democracies**
Low income	Burkina Faso; Burundi; Chad; Comoros; Congo, Dem. Rep.; Eritrea; The Gambia; Haiti; Lao, PDR; Liberia; Mauritania; Mozambique; Rwanda; Sudan; Togo; Uganda; Yemen, Rep.	Bangladesh; Benin; Central African Republic; Ethiopia; Guinea-Bissau; Madagascar; Malawi; Mali; Mozambique; Nepal; Niger; Nigeria; Senegal	Congo, Rep.; Kenya; Syrian Arab Republic	Cambodia; Ghana; Honduras; Lesotho; Tanzania; Zambia	Tajikistan; Vietnam	Moldova; Mongolia
Middle income	Algeria; Egypt, Arab Rep.; Iraq; Morocco; Pakistan	Djibouti; India; Nicaragua; Papua New Guinea	Cameroon; China; Equatorial Guinea; Libya; Swaziland; Tunisia; Zimbabwe	Albania; Bolivia; Botswana; Brazil; Dominican Republic; El Salvador; Guatemala; Indonesia; Iran, Islamic Rep.; Jamaica; Namibia; South Africa	Belarus; Cuba; Jordan; Kazakhstan; Uzbekistan	Armenia; Bulgaria; Colombia; Costa Rica; Ecuador; Fiji; Guyana; Latvia; Lithuania; Panama; Paraguay; Philippines; Romania; Russian Federation; Sri Lanka; Thailand; Ukraine; Venezuela, RB
High income	-	-	Bahrain; Kuwait; Oman; Qatar; Saudi Arabia; United Arab Emirates	Malaysia; Mauritius	Gabon	Argentian; Chile; Cyprus; Estonia; Israel; Slovenia; Trinidad and Tobago; Uruguay

Bibliography

Acemoglu, D. and J. Robinson (2008) Persistence of Power, Elites, Institutions. *American Economic Review* **98**, 267-293.

Acemoglu, D., S. Johnson, and J. Robinson (2001) The Colonial Origins of Comparative Advantage. *American Economic Review* **91**, 1369-1401.

Acemoglu, D., S. Johnson, and J. Robinson (2002) Reversal of Fortune: Geography and Institutions in the Making of the Modern World income Distribution. *Quarterly Journal of Economics* **117**, 1231-1294.

Acemoglu, D., S. Johnson, J. Robinson and P. Yared (2008) Income and Democracy. *American Economic Review* **98**, 808-842.

Alesina, A. and E. La Ferrara (2005) Ethnic Diversity and Economic Performance. *Journal of Economic Literature* **43**, 762-800.

Alesina, A. and D. Rodrik (1994) Distributive Politics and Economic Growth. *Quarterly Journal of Economics* **109**, 465-490.

Alesina, A., A. Devleeschauwer, W. Easterly, S. Kurlat, and R. Wacziarg (2003) Fractionalization. *Journal of Economic Growth* **8**, 155-194.

Alesina, A., R. Baquir, and W. Easterly (1999) Public Goods and Ethnic Divisions. *Quarterly Journal of Economics* **114**, 1243-1284.

Anderson, G. (2004) Making inference about the polarization, welfare and poverty of nations: A study of 101 countries from 1970 - 1995. *Journal of Applied Econometrics* **19**, 537–550.

Barro, R. (1991) Economic Growth in a Cross Section of Countries. *Quarterly Journal of Economics* **106**, 407-443.

Barro, R. and X. Sala-i-Martin (1991) Convergence across States and Regions. *Brookings Papers on Economic Activity* **1991**, 107–182.

Barro, R. and X. Sala-i-Martin (1992) Convergence. *Journal of Political Economy* **100**, 223–251.

Barro, R. (1996) Democracy and Growth. *Journal of Economic Growth* **1**, 1-27.

Barro, R. (1999) Determinants of Democracy. *Journal of Political Economy* **107**, 158-183.

Basu, S. and S. Jammalamadaka (2002) Unimodality in circular data: a Bayes test. In: N. Balakrishnan et al. (Eds.) *Advances on Methodological and Applied Aspects of Probability and Statistics* Taylor and Francis: New York, 141-153.

Beaudry, P., F. Collard, and D. Green (2005) Changes in the world distribution of output per worker, 1960–1998: How a standard decomposition tells us an unorthodox story. *Review of Economics and Statistics* **87**, 741–753.

Behboodian, J. (1970) On the modes of a mixture of two normal distributions. *Technometrics* **12**, 131–139.

Besley, T. and M. Kudamatsu (2006) Health and Democracy. *American Economic Review Papers and Proceedings* **96**, 313-315.

Besley, T. and R. Burgess (2002) The Political Economy of Government Responsiveness: Theory and Evidence from India. *Quarterly Journal of Economics* **117**, 1415-1451.

Bianchi, M. (1997) Testing for Convergence: Evidence from Non-Parametric Multimodality Tests. *Journal of Applied Econometrics* **12**, 393–409.

Blonigen, B. and W. Wilson (1999) Explaining Armington: what determines substitutability between home and foreign goods? *Canadian Journal of Economics* **32**, 1–21.

Boix, C. (2001) Democracy, Development, and the Public Sector. *American Journal of Political Science* **45**, 1-17.

Bourguignon, F. and C. Morrisson (2002) Inequality Among World Citizens: 1820-1992. *American Economic Review* **92**, 727–744.

Bourguignon, F. and T. Verdier (2000) Oligarchy, democracy, inequality and growth. *Journal of Development Economics* **62**, 285-313.

Broda, C., N. Limao and D. Weinstein (2009) Optimal Tariffs: The Evidence. *American Economic Review* forthcoming.

Busse, M. and H. Großmann (2007) The trade and fiscal impact of EU/ACP economic partnership agreements on West African countries. *Journal of Development Studies* **43**, 787–811.

Chen, H., J. Chen, and J. Kalbfleisch (2001) A modified likelihood ratio test for homogeneity in finite mixture models. *Journal of the Royal Statistical Society Series B* **63**, 19–29.

Chen, H., J. Chen, and J. Kalbfleisch (2004) Testing for a finite mixture model with two components. *Journal of the Royal Statistical Society Series B* **66**, 95–115.

Chen, J. and J. Kalbfleisch (2005) Modified likelihood ratio test in finite mixture models with a structural parameter. *Journal of Statistical Planning and Inference* **129**, 93–107.

Chen, S. and M. Ravallion (2004) How Have the World's Poorest Fared since the Early 1980s? *World Bank Research Observer* **19**, 141-169.

Chen, S. and M. Ravallion (2007) Absolute poverty measures for the developing world, 1981-2004. *World Bank Policy Research Working Paper* 4211.

Chernoff, H. (1954) On the distribution of the likelihood ratio. *Annals of Mathematical Statistics* **25**, 573–578.

Chotikapanich D., R. Valenzuela and P. Rao (1997) Global and regional inequality in the distribution of income: Estimation with limited and incomplete data. *Empirical Economics* **22**, 533-546.

Collier, P. (2001) Implications of ethnic diversity. *Economic Policy Analysis* **16**, 129-166.

Cronbach, L. (1987) Statistical tests for moderator variables: Flaws in analysis recently proposed. *Psychological Bulletin* **102**, 414-417.

Dacunha-Castelle, D. and E. Gassiat (1999) Testing the order of a model using locally conic parametrization: population mixtures and stationary ARMA processes. *Annals of Statistics* **27**, 1178–1209

Deaton, A. (2005) Measuring Poverty in a Growing World (or Measuring Growth in a Poor World. *Review of Economics and Statistics* **87**, 1-19.

Dowrick, S. and M. Akmal (2005) Contradicting Trends in Global Income Inequality: A Tale of Two Biases. *Review of Income and Wealth* **51**, 201–229.

Durlauf, S., P. Johnson, and J. Temple (2005) Growth econometrics. In: P. Aghion and S. Durlauf (Eds.) *Handbook of Economic Growth 1A* North-Holland: Amsterdam, 555-677.

Fan, Y. (1994) Testing the goodness of fit of a parametric density function by kernel method. *Econometric Theory* **10**, 316–356.

Fisher, N. and J. Marron (2001) Mode testing via the excess mass estimate. *Biometrika* **88**, 499–517.

Fisher, N., E. Mammen, and J. Marron (1994) Testing for multimodality. *Computational Statistics and Data Analysis* **18**, 499–512.

Fontagné, L., D. Laborde and C. Mitonitonne (2008) An Impact Study of the EU-ACP EPAs in the Six ACP Regions *CEPII Working Paper* 2008–04.

Fraley, C. and A. Raftery (2002) Model-based clustering, discriminant analysis, and density estimation. *Journal of the American Statistical Association* **97**, 611–631.

Franco, Á., C. Álvarez-Dardet, and M. Ruiz (2004) Effect of democracy on health: ecological study. *British Medical Journal* **329**, 1421-1423.

Gallaway, M., C. McDaniel and S. Rivera (2003) Short-run and Long-run Industry-level Estimates of U.S. Armington Elasticities. *North American Journal of Economics and Finance* **14**, 49–68.

Galor, O. (1996) Convergence? Inference from Theoretical Models. *The Economic Journal* **106**, 1056–1069.

Glaeser, E., G. Ponzetto, and A. Shleifer (2007) Why does democracy need education? *Journal of Economic Growth* **12**, 77-99.

Goffinet, B., P. Loisel, and B. Laurent (1992) Testing in normal mixture models when the proportions are known. *Biometrika* **79**, 842-846.

Gradstein, M. and B. Milanovic (2004) Does Liberté = Egalité? A Survey of the Empirical Links between Democracy and Inequality with some Evidence on the Transition Economies. *Journal of Economic Surveys* **18**, 515-537.

Graham, B. and J. Temple (2006) Rich nations, poor nations: how much can multiple equilibria explain? *Journal of Economic Growth* **11**, 5-41.

Grimm, M. and S. Klasen (2008) Geography vs. Institutions at the Village Level. *CESIFO Working Paper* 2259.

Grün, C. and S. Klasen (2008) Growth, Inequality, and Well-Being: Comparisons across Space and Time. *Oxford Economic Papers* **60**, 212-236.

Hall, P. and M. York (2001) On the calibration of Silverman's test for multimodality. *Statistica Sinica* **11**, 515–536.

Hall, R. and C. Jones (1999) Why Do Some Countries Produce So Much More Output Per Worker Than Others? *Quarterly Journal of Economics* **114**, 83-116.

Hartigan, J. and P. Hartigan (1985) The dip test of unimodality. *Annals of Statistics* **13**, 70–84.

Hathaway, R. (1985) A constrained formulation of maximum-likelihood estimation for normal mixture distributions. *Annals of Statistics* **13**, 795–800.

Hertel, T., D. Hummels, M. Ivanic and R. Keeney (2007) How Confident Can We Be in CGE-Based Assessments of Free Trade Agreements? *Economic Modelling* **24**, 611-635.

Hinkle, L. and M. Schiff (2004) Economic Partnership Agreements Between Sub-Saharan Africa and the EU: A Development Perspective. *The World Economy* **27**, 1321–1333.

Inglehart, R. and C. Welzel (2005) *Modernization, Cultural Change and Democracy. The Human Development Sequence.* New York: Cambridge University Press.

Jaccard, J., C. Wan, and R. Turrisi (1990) The Detection and Interpretation of Interaction Effects between Continuous Variables in Multiple Regression. *Multivariate Behavioral Research* **25**, 467-478.

Jones, C. (1997) On the Evolution of the World Income Distribution. *Journal of Economic Perspectives* **11**, 19–36.

Karingi, S., R. Lang, N. Oulmane, R. Perez, M. Jallab, and H. Hammouda (2005) Economic and Welfare Impacts of the EU-Africa Economic Partnership Agreements. *Economic Commission for Africa Working Paper* 10.

Kaufmann, D., A. Kraay, and M. Mastruzzi (2007) Governance Matters VI: Governance Indicators for 1996-2006. *World Bank Policy Research Working Paper* 4280.

Kee, H., A. Nicita, and M. Olarreaga (2004) Import Demand Elasticities and Trade Distorsions. *Review of Economics and Statistics* **90**, 666–682.

Keefer, P. and S. Khemani (2005) Democracy, Public Expenditure, and the Poor: Understanding Political Incentives for Providing Public Services. *World Bank Research Observer* **20**, 1-27.

Keribin, C. (2000) Consistent estimation of the order of mixture models. *Sankhyā Series A* **62**, 49–66.

Klasen, S. (2004) In Search of the Holy Grail: How to Achieve Pro Poor Growth? In: B. Tungodden, N. Stern, and I. Kolstad (Eds.) *Toward Pro Poor Policies - Aid, Institutions, and Globalization* New York: Oxford University Press, 63-94.

Knack, S. and P. Keefer (1995) Institutions and Economic Performance: Cross Country Tests Using Alternative Institutional Measures. *Economics and Politics* **7**, 207-27.

La Porta, R., F. López-de-Silanes, C. Pop-Eleches, and A. Shleifer (2004) Judicial Checks and Balances. *Journal of Political Economy* **112**, 445-470.

Le Gallo, J. (2004) Space-time analysis of GDP disparities among European regions: a Markov chain approach. *International Regional Science Review* **27**, 138–163.

Levine, R. and D. Renelt (1992) A Sensitivity Analysis of Cross-Country Growth Regressions. *American Economic Review* **82**, 942–963.

Li, P., J. Chen, and P. Marriott (2009) Non-finite Fisher information and homogeneity: the EM approach. *Biometrika* forthcoming.

Lipset, S. (1959) Some Social Requisites of Democray: Economic Development and Political Legitimacy. *American Political Science Review* **53**, 69-105.

Maasoumi, E., J. Racine, and T. Stengos (2007) Growth and convergence: A profile of distribution dynamics and mobility. *Journal of Econonmetrics* **136**, 483–508.

Mammen, E., J. Marron, and N. Fisher (1992) Some asymptotics for multimodality tests based on kernel density estimates. *Probability Theory and Related Fields* **91**, 115–132.

Mankiw, G., D. Romer and D. Weil (1992) A Contribution to the Empirics of Economic Growth. *Quarterly Journal of Economics* **107**, 407–437.

Mardia, K. and T. Sutton (1975) On the modes of a mixture of two von Mises distributions. *Biometrika* **62**, 699–701.

Marquez, J. (1990) Bilateral Trade Elasticities. *Review of Economics and Statistics* 72, 70–77.

Marquez, J. (1999) Long-Period Trade Elasticities for Canada, Japan, and the United States. *Review of International Economics* **7**, 102–116.

Marquez, J., (2002) *Estimating Trade Elasticities* New York: Springer.

Martyn, C. (2004) Commentary: Politics as a determinant of health. *British Medical Journal* **329**, 1423-1424.

McDonald, J. and A. Mantrala (1995) The Distribution of Personal Income: Revisited. *Journal of Applied Econometrics* **10**, 201-204.

McGuire M. and M. Olson (1996) The Economics of Autocracy and Majority Rule: The Invisible Hand and the Use of Force. *Journal of Economic Literature* **34**, 72-96.

Meltzer, A. and S. Richard (1981) A Rational Theory of the Size of Government. *Journal of Political Economy* **89**, 914-927.

Miguel, E. and M. Gugerty (2005) Ethnic Diversity, Social Sanctions, and Public Goods in Kenya. *Journal of Public Economics* **89**, 2325-2368.

Milanovic, B. (2002) True world income distribution, 1988 and 1993: First calculation based on household surveys alone. *Economic Journal* **112**, 51-92.

Milanovic, B. (2006) Global Income Inequality: What it is and Why it Matters. *World Bank Policy Research Working Paper* 3865.

Milner, C., O. Morrisey, and A. McKay (2005) Some Simple Analytics of the Trade and Welfare Effects of Economic Partnership Agreements. *Journal of African Economies* **14**, 327–358.

Minier, J. (1998) Democracy and Growth: Alternative Approaches. *Journal of Economic Growth* **3**, 241-66.

Müller, D. and G. Sawitzki (1991) Excess mass estimates and tests for multimodality. *Journal of the American Statistical Association* **86**, 738–746.

Olson, M. (1993) Dictatorship, Democracy, and Development. *American Political Science Review* **87**, 567-576.

Paap, R. and H. Dijk (1998) Distribution and mobility of wealth of nations. *European Economic Review* **42**, 1269–1293.

Persson, T. (2002) Do Political Institutions Shape Economic Policy. *Econometrica* **70**, 883-905.

Persson, T. and G. Tabellini (2000) *Political Economics. Explaining Economic Policy* Cambridge MA: MIT Press.

Persson, T. and G. Tabellini (2006) Democracy and Development: The Devil in Details. *American Economic Review Papers and Proceedings* **96**, 319-320.

Persson, T., G. Roland, and G. Tabellini (2000) Comparative Politics and Public Finance. *Journal of Political Economy* **108**, 1121-1161.

Peters, G. (2005) *Institutional Theory in Political Science* London/New York: Continuum.

Pittau, M. (2005) Fitting regional income distributions in the European Union. *Oxford Bulletin of Economics and Statistics* **67**, 135–161.

Pittau, M. and R. Zelli (2006) Empirical evidence of income dynamics across EU regions. *Journal of Applied Econometrics* **21**, 605–628.

Pritchett, L. and L. Summers (1996) Wealthier is Healthier. *Journal of Human Resources* **31**, 841-868.

Quah, D. (1996a) Convergence Empirics across Economies with (some) capital mobility. *Journal of Economic Growth* **1**, 95-124.

Quah, D. (1996b) Twin Peaks: Growth and Convergence in Models of Distribution Dynamics. *The Economic Journal* **106**, 1045–1055.

Quah, D. (1996c) Regional convergence clusters across Europe. *European Economic Review* **40**, 1353–1375.

Quah, D. (1997) Empirics for growth and distribution: polarization, stratification, and convergence clubs. *Journal of Economic Growth* **2**, 25–59.

Quah, D. (2002) One Third of the World's Growth and Inequality. *CEPR Discussion Paper* 3316.

Ravallion, M. (2003) The debate on globalization, poverty and inequality: why measurement matters. *World Bank Policy Research Working Paper* 3038.

Ravallion, M. and S. Chen (2003) Measuring pro-poor Growth. *Economic Letters* **78**, 93–99.

Ray, S. and B. Lindsay (2005) The topography of multivariate normal mixtures. *Annals of Statistics* **33**, 2042–2065.

Robertson, C. and J. Fryer (1969) Some descriptive properties of normal mixtures. *Skandinavisk Aktuarietidskrift* **69**, 137–146.

Rodrik. D. and R. Wacziarg (2005) Do Democratic Transitions produce Bad Economic Outcomes. *American Economic Review Papers and Proceedings* **95**, 50-54.

Romer, P. (1990) Endogenous Technological Change. *Journal of Political Economy* **98**, S71-S102.

Ross, M. (2006) Is Democracy Good for the Poor. *American Journal of Political Science* **50**, 860-874.

Sala-i-Martin, X. (1996) The Classic Approach to Convergence Analysis. *The Economic Journal* **106**, 1019–1036.

Sala-i-Martin, X. (2006) The World Distribution of Income: Falling Poverty and ... Convergence, Period. *Quarterly Journal of Economics* **121**, 351–397.

Sawyer, W. and R. Sprinkle (1999) *The Demand for Imports and Exports in the World Economy* Aldershot/London: Ashgate.

Self, S. and K.-Y. Liang (1987) Asymptotic properties of maximum likelihood estimators and likelihood ratio tests under nonstandard conditions. *Journal of the American Statistical Association* **82**, 605–610.

Sen, A. (1983) Development: Which Way Now? *Economic Journal* **93**, 745-762.

Sen, A. (1988) The Concept of Development. In: H. Chenery and T. Srinivasan (Eds.) *Handbook of Development Economics* Amsterdam: North Holland, 9-26.

Sen, A. (1991) Capability and Well-Being. In: M. Nussbaum and A. Sen (Eds.) *The Quality of Life* Oxford: Clarendon Press.

Sen, A. (1999a): *Development as Freedom.* Oxford: Oxford University Press.

Sen, A. (1999b): Democracy as a Universal Value. *Journal of Democracy* **10**, 3-17.

Sen, A. (2000) A Decade of Human Development. In: *Journal of Human Development* **1**, 17-23.

Sen, A. (2003) Development as Capability Expansion. In: S. Fukuda-Parr and A. Shiva Kumar (Eds.) *Readings in Human Development* New Delhi/New York: Oxford University Press, 41-58.

Sen, A. (2004) What's the Point of Democracy? *Bulletin of the American Academy of Arts and Sciences* **Spring 2004**, 8-11.

Shiells, C. and K. Reinert (1993) Armington Models and Terms-of-Trade Effects: Some Econometric Evidence for North America. *Canadian Journal of Economics* **26**, 299–316.

Shiells, C., R. Stern and A. Deardorff (1986) Estimates of the elasticities of substitution between imports and home goods for the United States. *Review of World Economics* **122**, 497–519.

Silverman, B. (1981) Using kernel density estimates to investigate multimodality. *Journal of the Royal Statistical Society Series B* **43**, 97–99.

Stasavage, D. (2005) Democracy and Education Spending in Africa. *American Journal of Political Science* **49**, 343-358.

Stern, R., J. Francis, and B. Schumacher (1976) *Price Elasticities in International Trade: An Annotated Bibliography*, London: Macmillan.

Tavares, J. and R. Wacziarg (2001) How democracy affects growth. *European Economic Review* **45**, 1341-1378.

Tsai, M. (2006) Does Political Democracy Enhance Human Development in Developing Countries. *American Journal of Economics and Sociology* **65**, 233-268.

Wand, M. and M. Jones (1995) *Kernel smoothing* London: Chapman and Hall.

Göttinger Studien zur Entwicklungsökonomik
Göttingen Studies in Development Economics

Herausgegeben von/Edited by Hermann Sautter
und/and Stephan Klasen

Die Bände 1-8 sind über die Vervuert Verlagsgesellschaft (Frankfurt/M.) zu beziehen.

Bd./Vol. 9 Hermann Sautter / Rolf Schinke (eds.): Social Justice in a Market Economy. 2001.

Bd./Vol.10 Philipp Albert Theodor Kircher: Poverty Reduction Strategies. A comparative study applied to empirical research. 2002.

Bd./Vol.11 Matthias Blum: Weltmarktintegration, Wachstum und Innovationsverhalten in Schwellen ländern. Eine theoretische Diskussion mit einer Fallstudie über „Argentinien 1990-1999". 2003.

Bd./Vol.12 Jan Müller-Scheeßel: Die Privatisierung und Regulierung des Wassersektors. Das Beispiel Buenos Aires/Argentinien. 2003.

Bd./Vol.13 Ludger J. Löning: Economic Growth, Biodiversity Conservation, and the Formation of Human Capital in a Developing Country. 2004.

Bd./Vol.14 Silke Woltermann: Transitions in Segmented Labor Markets. The Case of Brazil. 2004.

Bd./Vol.15 Jörg Stosberg: Political Risk and the Institutional Environment for Foreign Direct Investment in Latin America. An Empirical Analysis with a Case Study on Mexico. 2005.

Bd./Vol.16 Derk Bienen: Die politische Ökonomie von Arbeitsmarktreformen in Argentinien. 2005.

Bd./Vol.17 Dierk Herzer: Exportdiversifizierung und Wirtschaftswachstum. Das Fallbeispiel Chile. 2006.

Bd./Vol.18 Jann Lay: Poverty and Distributional Impact of Economic Policies and External Shocks. Three Case Studies from Latin America Combining Macro and Micro Approaches. 2007.

Bd./Vol.19 Kenneth Harttgen: Empirical Analysis of Determinants, Distribution and Dynamics of Poverty. 2007.

Bd./Vol. 20 Stephan Klasen / Felicitas Nowak-Lehmann: Poverty, Inequality and Migration in Latin America. 2008.

Bd./Vol. 21 Isabel Günther: Empirical Analysis of Poverty Dynamics. With Case Studies from Sub-Saharan Africa. 2007.

Bd./Vol. 22 Peter Dung: Malaysia und Indonesien: Wirtschaftliche Entwicklungsstrategien in zwei Vielvölkerstaaten. 2008.

Bd./Vol. 23 Thomas Otter: Poverty, Income Growth and Inequality in Paraguay During the 1990s. Spatial Aspects, Growth Determinants and Inequality Decomposition. 2008.

Bd./Vol. 24 Mark Misselhorn: Measurement of Poverty, Undernutrition and Child Mortality. 2008.

Bd./Vol. 25 Julian Weisbrod: Growth, Poverty and Inequality Dynamics. Four Empirical Essays at the Macro and Micro Level. 2008.

Bd./Vol. 26 Johannes Gräb: Econometric Analysis in Poverty Research. With Case Studies from Developing Countries. 2009.

Bd./Vol. 27 Sebastian Vollmer: A Contribution to the Empirics of Economic and Human Development. 2009.

www.peterlang.de

MIX
Papier | Fördert gute Waldnutzung
FSC® C083411

Kolibri 360 GmbH
Ferdinand-Jühlke-Straße 7
99095 Erfurt, Deutschland
produktsicherheit@kolibri360.de